SEVEN AND A HALF STEPS TOWARD FINANCIAL FREEDOM

As Taught By a Practical Ancient Egyptian Sage

A Reader's Theater Script combined with Narrative Non-Fiction Discussions

By: Diane D Koster

Seven and a Half Steps Toward Financial Freedom: As Taught by a Practical Ancient Egyptian Sage

By: Diane D Koster Published by Amazon.com – KDP

info@rforcc.com

Cover by Diane D Koster

In Memory of
My mother, Jo Ann, and my step-father, Alfred,
who helped me develop an unfailing work ethic.

I also want to thank those who read this script while I was writing it and gave me invaluable suggestions – especially, Tracy Eisenhart for using it with her classes and reporting back to me.

How to Use this Book

By the week
The lessons the main character, Kheruef, gives are meant to be done once weekly. He tells his students what he'd like them to learn and what experience he'd like them to have to understand it. Then he tells them to go do it. You are welcome to take this book and parse it weekly!

On the other hand, if you want to read it all at once, have at it. It will probably feel like a bunch of other books you've consumed in one sitting but, hey, you're welcome to do it at your own pace. Fast … or slow!

Group of Friends
One way to tackle these concepts is together with a group of friends. There are at least 20 roles, from simple one or two lines to the granddaddy of them all – the rich man, "Kheruef," and the "Reading Readers", the Narrator and Readers.

There are conversations between two or three people at the end of a lesson, or there is the lesson itself where Kheruef explains the concept and then "assigns homework." So, gather your friends around you, or ZOOM it together, and make it a book club night. With assignments.

Reading alone
No biggee. I like to read alone, too. Sometimes when I reread the book to check for consistency, or I think I should add something to clarify a point, I read it like I'm all of the characters. For me, I know what I intended by creating these characters so, it's not hard to "be" all of them. So – You be you and everybody else, too!

Classroom with Worksheets
Really? I wrote this for my class! Only, I retired before I finished the book, so I only got to hear some of it read by my students.

If you're using this, be sure to check out *Appendix A* of questions and prompts for most sections. And, more power to you. I frequently got questions from my students like: Why don't they teach us about real life in school? Why doesn't anyone explain how we should take care of our money once we get it?

When I asked what these meant, inevitably it revolved around money and what to do with it. Surprisingly, I had a number of students who never got paid an allowance of actual cash. They got paid in "return favors" (mom would get them something for their chores) and occasionally, someone got to use a card (dad would say to use the card and hand it back when they were done! YIKES!!) So, certain kids are going to need more help figuring out some of this than others. True story.

NOTE: When using this with students, be aware that one chapter deals with drinking beer. In assessing Needs vs Wants, the characters (after Kheruef's lesson) debate what is the best way to drink beer. At no time do they drink to get drunk. Beer was a common source of liquid in ancient Egypt and adults and children consumed it daily. It had far less alcohol in it than we have nowadays, and what alcohol that was in the beer killed water-borne pathogens.

Table of Contents

Seven and a Half Steps Toward Financial Freedom As Taught By a Practical Ancient Egyptian Sage

# of Lines	Roles
Throughout	Readers and Narrators – however you'd like to divide them up!
	Ruling Class
4	SITAYET – Main Vizier to PTOLEMY
7	PTOLEMY – Pharaoh of Egypt
	Richest Man
LOTS	Kheruef – [unflappable] The Sage on the Stage
	Students in Kheruef's class
10	Enlil – Baker, owner of a bakery
16	Lugal - Scribe
10	Qishti – [impertinent/haughty] – Makes fine robes for PTOLEMY's men
16	Nadin – Butcher
17	Aya – *woman* – Weaves blankets and sail cloth
12	Kammani – *woman* – Weaves fine cloth
18	Puzu – Raises sheep to sell wool to weavers
18	Ninkurra – *woman* - Makes pottery – cups, plates
16	Marduk – Makes shields – from copper and hides
20	Ishtar- Makes sharp stone knives, copper knives and scrapers
9	Elutil – *woman* – Makes clothes for all but sometimes the pharaoh's daughters
25	Taram – *woman* – [practical] Raises chickens, ducks, and geese for eggs
16	Nammu – Builds homes and furniture
14	Delondra – *woman* – Tends cows for milk to sell to cheesemakers
4	Belessunu – Creates jewelry for Ptolemy's family, and wigs
2 - 9	Others – Seller 1, Seller 2, Farmer, Woman, and Aria

The roles could just as easily be male or female, but there are places where Kheruef says something archaic like, "Good woman." In order to keep those instances from causing problems in a classroom or reading circle, it's just easier to assign the specific female roles to … females, or whoever can handle the gender jump.

The names are from data banks that give actual names recorded in the historical record of "Egyptian names" and "Mesopotamian names."

The number for the amount of lines is given to teachers or groups so that you may decide who might be best suited for a lot or a little reading. Most lines are not very long. That said, plenty of them are long! And ALL of the workers should try to get involved in ALL. Sometimes it's a motion – nodding, and sometimes it's a laugh – hahaha!

Reader's Theater Play written by: Diane D. Koster

Modeled after: "The Richest Man in Babylon" by George Samuel Clason in 1926

The Richest Man In Egypt – The Seven and a Half Steps

SITAYET: **For years, your people worked and built your majesty's great irrigation canals and mighty temples to the gods. They made plenty of money and they were happy. Now that all of that work is finished, the people seem unable to support themselves in the way they once enjoyed. Some of the workers are unemployed and don't know what to do to help themselves. Some of the farmers are unsure of how to sell or trade what they grow and produce. And, many don't have enough money to buy food!**

PTOLEMY: **Where has all the money gone that we paid them with?**

SITAYET: **It filtered through the fingers of most of our people as quickly as cow's milk goes through a strainer. Now that you aren't paying them anymore, most of your people have nothing to show for their earnings.**

PTOLEMY: **Why are there only a few people who have something to show for all their hard work?**

SITAYET: **Because they know how to handle their money! You can't condemn a person who knows how to make his money work for him!**

PTOLEMY: **So … who knows best, in all our city, how to make that money work for him? Who can teach the people how to do what he does?**

SITAYET: **Who is the richest man in Egypt, you are asking? Besides you, of course.**

PTOLEMY: **That man is Kheruef! He is the richest man in Egypt. Bring him to me tomorrow morning.**

The following day, Kheruef goes before Ptolemy.

PTOLEMY: **Is it true that you're the richest man in Egypt?**

KHERUEF: **Yes! That's what people say!**

PTOLEMY: **How did you get so wealthy?**

KHERUEF: **I took advantage of opportunities when they became available. I had nothing to start with and I figured out how to make my money work for me.**

***PTOLEMY:* Ever since we stopped paying for the city's improvements, many of the people of Egypt have been unable to help themselves make a living. I was wondering if you could teach them how to do what you did.**

***KHERUEF:* I am your humble servant. I will make every effort to teach people the seven steps for a heavy purse. Send those people who are already employed and who have a desire to learn to the Great Temple of Hapi - that the things I will teach them will come to them like the gracious flood from the Nile.**

Historical Note: During the reign of Ptolemy, actual coins were in use, probably for taxes and daily use.

ANNOUNCEMENT! LET IT BE KNOWN THAT ONE OF THE RICHEST MEN IN EGYPT WILL TEACH THOSE WHO WILL COME TO HIS CLASSES TO LEARN HIS SECRETS OF GAINING WEALTH!

The First Step
Save One in Ten

At the Great Temple of Hapi

ENLIL– **Behold! The richest man in Egypt looks the same as you and me! He walks on two feet!**

LUGAL **– He does! This better be good.**

KHERUEF: **The GREAT PTOLEMY has asked me to teach you how to become rich. I started the same way you all have. I was poor and mostly my purse was empty. I taught myself how to save and make money and I will teach you to do the same. However, while I can teach you, if you have bad habits and you can't break those habits, then I can't say whether you'll ever be rich. Just having your ears listen isn't the key to getting rich. I need you to say that, yes, you understand what I just said. Do you understand that simply listening isn't enough?**

ALL: **Yes.**

QISHTI: **What if I don't like what you say?**

KHERUEF nods: **Then, you don't have to do anything! But you may not find a way to get rich!**

QISHTI shrugged.

KHERUEF looked at everyone and pulled out his purse.: **The first storehouse of my money is my purse. I hated its emptiness. I desired it to be full of coins! I looked for all the remedies I could find and I found seven. I will explain one of the steps - One idea for each of the next 7 weeks,. You may ask me questions and we can even debate why the step works. Today, I will teach you the first step. Now hear this. No man can climb this mountain of wealth, if he cannot step firmly on this first step. Therefore, you must have a job and a source of income.**

KHERUEF addressed a thoughtful man in the second row: **My good man, what do you do for a living?**

LUGAL: **I am a scribe and I write the town's records on clay tablets.**

KHERUEF: **I had that very same job at the beginning! I earned my first coins that way – so, I think you can become rich like me!**

KHERUEF to NADIN **– And, sir, what do you do to earn your coins?**

NADIN **– I am a meat butcher. I buy the cows the farmers raise and I kill them and sell the meat to the wives and banquet planners and the hides to the sandal makers.**

KHERUEF to NADIN: **You have every advantage and will likely succeed as I have.**

KHERUEF then addressed AYA: **Good woman, tell us what you do.**

AYA (woman): **I weave thick warm blankets to keep the people warm in winter, and lightweight coverings to shield the people from the mosquitos and flies in the summer. I also make sail cloth.**

AYA turned her attention to the woman next to her – the woman had her head covered with a veil and her face down: **And this, is my very good friend, Kammani. She weaves the finest cloth in all the land so that the people may wear comfortable clothing all year round.**

KHERUEF: **Can she not speak for herself?**

KAMMANI (woman) holds her head down and AYA continues to speak: **She shies from attention, kind sir. When she was yet young, she was burned by some flaming door coverings as she tried to escape her home. She lost her family when her house was blackened. She was raised by her grandmother who taught her the finest weaving and the most intricate needlework.**

KHERUEF nodded: **We forget that the person on the inside is not necessarily the person on the outside. I'm glad you both are here.**

KHERUEF continued to listen to all the men and women present.
KHERUEF addressed every man and woman there and their jobs and livelihoods varied.

PUZU: **I raise a few sheep, but mostly goats and I cut the wool off to sell to the spinners and weavers and wigmakers.**

NINKURRA: **I make every day pottery, plates and cups. People come to me when they break something, which, sir, is often!**

ALL laugh.

MARDUK: (speaks with a thick accent) **I make copper and tough hide shields for Ptolemy's guards.**

ISHTAR: **I make sharp stone knives and scrapers which I sell to the butchers.**

ELUTIL (woman): **I make clothes, sometimes for us all, and sometimes for the maidens in the court of Ptolemy.**

ENLIL: **I grind the grain and run one of the bread bakeries in town.**

QISHTI stands haughtily: **I make Ptolemy's court their fine robes and garments.**

TARAM (woman): **I raise chickens, geese and ducks and collect the eggs to sell at market.**

NAMMU: **I build the homes and furniture for the people.**

DELONDRA (woman): **I tend the cows and milk them and sell the milk to the cheese and yogurt makers.**

BELESSUNU: **I make beautiful jewelry for Ptolemy's family and friends, as well as weave wigs from fine linen thread and hair.**

KHERUEF: said to them all: **My students, you can see that there are many trades and jobs. Each of you has an income according to the job you do – some have a lot of money coming in all at once that you must give out in large amounts, and some of you have a steady stream of coins that flows all the time. Isn't that right?**

ALL: (nodding) **Yes.**

KHERUEF: **And each of you desire a fatter purse, yes?!**

ALL: (laughing) **Yes!!!**

KHERUEF: **So, if each of you wants to build a fortune for himself, it only makes sense that you use the money that you have, right?**

ALL: (some sighs) **Yes.**

***KHERUEF:* *looked at TARAM – the raiser of chickens.* Good woman, what would happen if every day you collect 10 eggs into a basket, but by the end of the day, you only sell nine. You take that one egg and place it in a separate basket. And the next day you do the same with your market basket …and the next day and the next day….**

***TARAM:* Soon, the separate basket will be overflowing with the extra eggs.**

***KHERUEF:* Why?**

***TARAM:* Because each day I will put in one more egg than I take out and I will add that to the separate basket. So, soon, the separate basket will be overly full.**

***KHERUEF smiles and seems to change the subject:* Does anyone here have an empty purse?**

ALL laugh and some wave their empty or nearly empty purses.

***KHERUEF:* All right! Now I will tell you the first step. For every ten coins you put in your purse, take out and use only nine. Then put that one coin someplace safe at the end of the day. Do the same thing the next day. For every ten, use only nine… and so on. Your savings will start to fatten just as the extra basket gathered more eggs – one at a time.**

ALL - Some people grumble, some nod

***KHERUEF:* Don't make fun of this simple exercise. The Truth is always simple! I told you that this is how I built my fortune. In the beginning, I too, carried an empty purse and I cursed its emptiness. But, before too long, after I started saving, I could see coins came to me more easily. And I kept more for myself!**

***NADIN:* But that means I won't be able to go to the pub and have a beer with my friends.**

***KHERUEF:* That's true. Your actions speak loudly. You spend money on things you find important. If becoming rich isn't important, then you won't save. And you'll never get rich! It's your choice. If you choose differently, then you may someday become rich!**

Men and women start talking among themselves and debating what was said.
***KHERUEF waited a bit and then interrupted.:* Everyone! Here is the strange truth that I discovered. When I stopped paying out more than nine tenths of my earnings per day, I managed along just as well! For some reason, I learned quickly how to live without using that coin! Soon, my extra purse easily held the coins I had saved and I didn't feel compelled to spend them. Consider what you desire the most. Gold and**

wealth? or a beer every day? more land? or a mug of coffee every morning? fattening your herds with more animals? Or, an extra piece of bread at lunch every day?

KHERUEF spoke clearly: **Your first assignment is to return with the coins that you save after this lesson. We'll continue to talk and debate about this in a week.**

The room got noisier as groups talked, debated and then, left until the next week.

Aya and Kammani were last out, waiting until the others had left so no one would stare. At least, that's what they thought. At their backs, behind the statue of Hapi, the richest man watched as all his students left, including the mysterious woman. He bowed to their backs and exited the room.

AYA: **What did you think of the talk today? Should we return next week?**

KAMMANI: **(*A bit of a lilt in her voice*) I think we should experiment this week. Let's challenge each other to see who can save a coin or two! Let's make it a sort of game!**

AYA: **(*laughing*) What does the winner get for this game? We can't very well give the money we saved away!**

KAMMANI: **Let's think of something. What if the Winner gets to sit for a day while the other has to do all of the chores?**

AYA: **Foof! That would be a LOT of WORK!!.**

KAMMANI: **Okay – what do you think should be the winner's take?**

AYA: **I think I'd like the winner to be served the finest dinner that we can make. 3 courses. With some vegetables from the garden, a bit of meat that we've saved, a glass of wine, and a sweet dessert.**

KAMMANI: **Hahaha! You and your desserts! That's what you're really waiting for!**

AYA: **You know me too well. What do you think? If I lose, I could make your favorite dinner.**

KAMMANI: **(*thoughtful*) We hardly indulge ourselves in foods, so maybe that dinner is just what we need to help us save our coins. Deal! Is it still good for you?**

AYA: **Yes! It's a deal!**

The women chatted as they made their way home. On reaching their abode they both went to their separate corners and looked to find their spare change purse. Each made a special spot to hide the purse, careful to make sure the other hadn't observed them. They were ready for Kheruef's challenge.

The next morning, they arose and ate their simple breakfast of boiled lentils with chopped dates stirred in along with some bread and beer. Then they cleaned up and went into their workroom.

Since the two of them shared the plot of land, they had built a spacious workroom with thick walls and benches on the sides. Toward the left side sat Aya's large loom for weaving coverings. On her benches she had yarns of several colors and some coarsely spun flax. Merchants often bought her cloth to use as shade for stands at the markets. Occasionally, boat builders bought the flaxen cloth for sails. In fact, the ceiling to their weaving room was several layers of her cloth ... enough to block the direct sun but also allow light in the room.

On the right, Kammani's two looms were smaller. On her benches lay balls of the finest spun flax. With these, she made a delicate linen cloth for the best clothing. Priests from the nearby temples often came to see her with their requests for themselves, or for dressing the statues of the gods and goddesses in the temples.

Assistants picked up bowls of water and walked around the room, sprinkling the walls and saying their morning thanks to the Gods. They pulled the cloths from the doorways and soaked them in water and then put the cloths back up in the doorway. The temperature dropped in the room and they would work in comfort, until lunch. Then they would sprinkle the walls and soak the cloth in the doorways again, have lunch and work for a few more hours until the room had become unbearably warm.

Today, the women started their work with a conversation about the "saving coins challenge".

***AYA:* Have you thought about our deal anymore? How you're going to cook me my favorite dinner?**

***KAMMANI:* You mean the meal you will fix for me? *(laughs with a sweet lilt to her voice)* Truly, whoever wins will be a win for both of us since we eat together, but still ... yes, I have been thinking about it.**

***AYA:* I have a customer coming today to see about some sail cloth. I shall remember to put my coins away and then save one out of every ten! IF I can. I need to buy more flax thread!**

KAMMANI: **Yes. I keep thinking about that. We've always been frugal. We spend most of what we have on what we need to create our cloth. I can't imagine where the surplus money will come from!**

AYA: **I know. It worries me, too. *(She pauses)* We could raise our prices ever so slightly. And, then promise ourselves to put the extra earned away.**

KAMMANI: **That's a good idea. But, I don't want to overprice my goods. There are plenty of weavers out there in our city!**

AYA: **There are many who make sail cloth like me. But not so many who make your fine linen for clothing. *(Aya sniffed sadly.)***

KAMMANI: **Oh … Aya. We will figure something out. In the meantime, we will try our hardest to save some coins. We can do this! Think of all the obstacles we have overcome. Saving a few coins should be easy!**

They worked in silence. Their assistants bustled about adding new thread and changing places with co-workers. After lunch, before the room had gotten too hot, the sail cloth buyer came. Aya bargained with the buyer and wouldn't budge on her final price. Finally, the buyer agreed with the price, took his cloth and left.

AYA: **I wasn't asking that much more, but it made the bargaining all that much harder for me! Still, I did get a few more coins.**

KAMMANI: **I heard! You were so brave. Perhaps this saving will make us not give in so often and we'll be able to make more money so we can save.**

AYA: **When will the priests be by to get more cloth?**

KAMMANI: **Before three days' time. I still have a few more folds of cloth to make, so I'll be working hard until then. I must be strong like you!**

AYA: **You are such a good friend!**

For the rest of the week, the women made good on their promise to save coins AND to bargain harder for the worth of their cloth. In the end, they had tied – each had brought in 15 coins that they were able to save. So, they made a bigger dinner than normal for the both of them. Not so much as to waste food, but just enough to make them smile at the sweet desserts that completed the meal.

Historical Notes:
Meals in ancient Egypt were generally vegetables from their small gardens, onions, and lentils. For proteins they ate some fish, birds, eggs, and very rarely, some sort of meat (goat or sheep). IF things were sweetened, they used dates, honey and figs. The would buy bread from vendors in the markets because owning a large oven was costly to run, though many bought flour and made a common kind of flatbread.

Evaporative cooling had been known about since ancient Persia (400 BC - yakhchal). In addition to wetting the walls, the Egyptians would hang damp cloths or hang wet reeds in the doorways. Just inside the doorway, where a breeze was likely to flow, they placed wide water filled bowls on the floors so the breeze blowing through the room would pick up the moisture, thereby cooling the room.

Egyptian women were way ahead of their ancient counterparts as far as human rights. They had many of the same legal rights as men. They could own property, run businesses (typically make up, creams, perfume and clothing) and represent themselves in a legal court. Wealthy women could attend school and become scribes, priestesses, dentists and doctors.

Generalization:

How might a person save one in ten coins today?

Let's take a simple example first. Your next door neighbor asks you to run an errand, say to go the store for milk. She says she'll give you $5.00 when you return. You go, get the milk, and get your reward/payment/"coins" or cash from her.

The math behind one in ten simply means 1/10th or 10 percent. When you divide $5.00 by 10, or multiply it by .10 (for the 10%) you come up with 50 cents, or .50. If you were staying true to your desire to save, you would spend some of the money and save the change, or ask someone to "break" the five dollar bill for you into $4.00 and a dollar in change (4 quarters). Then, you'd take the 2 quarters (50 cents) and stash them away.

Another example might go like this. You earn in a pay period (one week, two weeks, or one month) $1,000 dollars. Again, you would divide it by 10 or multiply it by .10. The answer is $100. If you were trying to save, you would put that $100 somewhere safe.

Somewhere safe: Just exactly where is "someplace safe" in this economy?

Simple: Many people in the United States have a Coin Jar, or a tin, that they keep change in. Or, you could save it the old fashioned way and get yourself a piggy bank. Others, simply throw the change into a drawer. Change has become less important in our daily transactions and so, many people inadvertently "save" change without thinking about it. Some even put one dollar bills in the jar rolled up tightly. Or, if they get a dollar coin as change, they just toss that it in, too, regardless of how many they keep. Then, when the ice cream truck drives around, many a kid or an adult will remember their saved coins!! For the purposes of saving 1/10th, however, the object would be to put the money in the jar and leave it until later and NOT run out to get ice cream!!

Time spent wisely: Once you start accumulating money, it will probably be important to have a checking and savings account. This will allow you to get a debit card and to not have lots of high end dollars stashed away where they could be easily stolen.

When you start a checking account, be sure that you use your savings account – by putting money in it that you won't use unless you absolutely have to. Banks now have an online presence and will allow you to move your own money between the checking and savings accounts. Imagine then, that you go to the bank or teller/ATM machine and deposit your money into your account. Later, at home, you want to figure out what 1/10th or 10 percent is. I imagine, at this point, you would remember to divide the amount by 10 or multiply by .10. If we do this with a paycheck for one week of $365.23, we would come up with $36.52. <u>(Notice all we really had to do was move the decimal point one place to the left and drop off the last number.)</u> You would go to your online banking account, and go to a transaction called "Transfer". You would choose to TAKE the money ($36.52) <u>from</u> your checking account and to PUT IT <u>into</u> your savings account. That would leave 9/10ths of your paycheck ($328.71) still IN your checking account for use.

Simpler than above, but perhaps not as wise: Many employers now have direct deposit. The money actually never gets INTO your hands and you don't really see it. It's wonderful, in oh-so-many ways. However, it's also easy to become disconnected to your income. You won't actually SEE the amount UNLESS you go online. If you would rather NOT go online, many banks allow for automatic transfers of some money. Let's say you decide to have $50.00 transferred every month. That amount represents 10% of $500. If you ONLY earn $500 per month EVERY month, then, great! If there are times when you earn MORE – then $50 isn't enough. If you earn LESS, then $50.00 could hurt your ability to pay the bills!

If you were serious about putting away 10%, you would really have to go online and do it manually. I haven't run into a bank that will let you manage the specific percentage taken out of your paycheck automatically. There are a few banks that have "summer accounts" where they put a percentage aside for say, teachers. So, maybe there are some banks who have a "10% Paycheck Balance Transfer". Be sure that the automated transfer doesn't cost you a bank charge!

The Characters: Kammani and Aya are good examples of a supportive relationship. They challenge each other to save, but the cost of losing isn't the money they saved! They happen to be roommates and they are aware of each other's business endeavors. Still, they are not overly competitive so that they feel they must cheat each other or themselves. They talk about the challenge throughout the week, and how they might meet it, thereby keeping the goal in mind.

The Second Step
Needs and Wants

KHERUEF nods and smiles and his students file into the room.
KHERUEF: **So, how did you do? Can someone ask a question related to last week's experience?**

ELUTIL stood: **How can I keep one coin in 10 when all the coins in my purse are not enough to pay for all of my expenses?**

KHERUEF: **Everyone here needs to make sure that you are not confusing what is necessary with what you desire. Many of you have families and you need to feed them. But your earnings can only go so far. Clearly seeing the things that you don't HAVE TO HAVE is important. There are many things we LIKE TO HAVE. When you see a handsome pair of shoes at the market, ask, Do I really NEED new shoes? When you see a cute toy for your daughter ask, Does she NEED this new toy? When you see a nice scarf that would look good on your wife, Does she NEED that new scarf? If you have some excellent bread from the vendor, Do you NEED another piece? Your choice to spend your money is the burden of desire. Did you see your neighbor add a room onto his house … and now you think you should too?**

ALL - Some grumble, some nod their heads, some say: Yes.

KHERUEF: **Let me tell you! If a farmer doesn't tend to the growing crops, weeds will spring up between them and steal the water meant for the crops. Desires do the same to men. I may want to travel farther than I usually do, but there are limits. There are limits to my time, my strength, the distance I can go and to the over-the-top happiness I can have. I say to you – if you do not weed the crops, if you do not tell yourself you can't have everything you see, you will find that you will never be gratified because there will always be one more thing you think you MUST have. But you don't have to have everything that another has!**

BELESSUNU Looks around at everyone : **I see greed around me every day. As soon as I make one person a beautiful necklace, another wants the same … only better. Are we all like that only about different things?**

ISHTAR : **I have seen that too. If I make a knife for someone, his neighbor may soon come and ask for that same knife. But for me, the stone doesn't always break the same way, so I often make a special knife for someone that they end up not wanting because it's not the exact same!**

***ENLIL*:** **I think this must be true. I make breads and if one piece is just a bit smaller than the one I just sold, buyers will spend a lot of time looking amongst my bread slices for that same size.**

Men and women nod and look at each other slightly embarrassed.

KHERUEF: **Good! You are beginning to see what your desires have caused! You feel you must feed your desires as well as feeding the feeling of getting as much or better than the next person! Study your living habits and your thoughts. If you can, put on a clay tablet the thing that you desire most. Consider the smaller desires that you will need to ignore and save the necessary coins for the greater desire. Adjust as you need, but continue to save one in ten coins and on good days, save an extra coin! Keep your goal in mind!**

QISHTI: **If I see something I want, I get it. I am worth it!!**

KHERUEF: **Are you not worth the life of a rich man? If you already have enough money, then surely this class isn't for you. But if you came because you are not as rich as your clients, then perhaps you will need to decide which goal is more important. To eat well and live loud? Or to save and live a long, wealthy life?**

AYA: **I found that just having my saved money in my purse as I shopped was a reason to spend! I took a few coins with me just to look for fresh fruit at the market, but when I saw the honeyed sweets which are my favorite, I went directly to that vendor and bought one! Sweet things are my weakness! How do I stop myself??**

KHERUEF: (smiling) **I know what you mean! Self-discipline is the hardest task! Bread always stole my money!!! Call out the things that steal your money and we shall see that we all have work to do !!**

NADIN and PUZU: **BEER! (they look at each other and laugh)**

MARDUK: **Date cakes!**

NINKURRA: **Hand Creams!**

DELONDRA: **Pomegranates!**

ELUTIL: **Earrings!**

NAMMU: **Strong sandals!**

KHERUEF: **Wait. Nammu. Do you not need strong shoes to do your business?**

NAMMU: (looks at the ground) **Yes. But I have so many strong sandals now, that I'm afraid they are stealing my money. When I first started building homes, I remember having to work with broken down shoes. So, when I started making money, I always looked for stronger and stronger sandals. I'm afraid I have more than I need now, yet I still look.**

KHERUEF: **I understand how that happened. And, you are right. Now they are stealing your money. Today, you have noticed this, and you can change it. Breaking old habits will be hard, but when habits cost us money and steal our earnings, we must be strong. The next time you are at a market and the sandals catch your attention, find out how much a pair costs and go home directly. Put that same money in your safe spot. It will be as if the sandals are paying you back!!**

KHERUEF clears his throat: **Everyone, your attention. Your second step is to watch for those things that steal your money – especially for a short term gain. Start asking yourself: Am I really thirsty? Am I truly hungry? Do I NEED this or do I just WANT this? What will this do for me and my goal if I buy it? You want to have coins for the true necessities, and then, only lastly, to pay for the enjoyments and to gratify your desires.** *[he nods at QISHTI and then looks at everyone.]* **But remember, do all this while saving your extra coins. And, that means, Aya!!** *(he gets her attention)* **Don't put those extra coins in your purse if you truly mean to save them.** *[he smiles at Aya and pauses]* **You can't spend what you don't have with you. We will meet next week for the third step.**

Nadin and Puzu stepped out together into the bright sunshine of the clear Egyptian day.

NADIN: **So, do you have a favorite pub?**

PUZU: **I was about to ask you the same. I like my beer a little cool, so I go to the Cave in the Hill just up from the market area. The owner built his shop with the regular mud bricks, but dug back into the hill. It keeps the area cool.**

NADIN: **Is that so? I go to Market on the third day of every week. Aladdin's Beer Stop is a fast and easy way to grab a quick thirst quencher. Many people shop there to get their beer for the week. Aladdin sells crocks filled with his brew and he takes the empty crocks in return for a discount.**

PUZU: **I see we drink for different reasons. You should come up with me sometime and I'll show you how to drink beer slowly.**

NADIN: **(smiling) And you should accompany me and we'll see who can drink the beer the fastest!!**

PUZU: **Alright! Third day of the week! I'll meet you at Aladdin's and from there we'll go to the Cave in the Hill!**

NADIN: **It's a deal!!**

They parted ways. On the third day of the week, Nadin and Puzu met up at Aladdin's Beer Stop.

NADIN: **Good to see you, Puzu! Watch how he conducts business. On one side his son serves individual glasses for a few coins. On the other, Aladdin trades out full crocks for empty crocks. Let's get in line over here.**

PUZU: **How many coins?**

NADIN: **Two! It's cheap!**

PUZU: **(looking in his purse) I will have just enough for one drink more at the Cave.**

Nadin and Puzu bought their cups. They looked at each other and Nadin gave the signal.

NADIN: **To wet your tongue! GO!**

The two started drinking and Nadin won – having practiced! It took all of 20 seconds.

PUZU: **Burrrrp! (He laughed)**

NADIN: **Burrp! (Laughing, too)**

PUZU: **It was refreshing, but now it's gone! I usually like to enjoy my beer to make it last longer.**

NADIN: **Then, let's head up to the Cave!**

The two men made small talk as they walked up the hill, through the dampened cloth doors and into a small, shady, and cooler hut. A servant walked around the room watering the walls. Around the walls were built-in benches. They waited for their eyes to adjust to the light and headed to the serving area.

PUZU: **Now, wait and follow my lead on drinking. You will have to slow down to drink with me!**

They each paid another 2 coins for a slightly smaller drinking cup.

NADIN: **This is hardly enough to wet my tongue, yet it costs the same!**

PUZU: **True. But remember to follow my lead on this. You will have longer refreshment for the same money. I promise.**

The men took their drinks to the benches. Puzu took a sip and looked at Nadin.

NADIN: **A sip? Okay then.**

Nadin took a sip and rolled the beer around in his mouth. He looked at Puzu, who had done something similar only he was squeezing his tongue to the roof of his mouth with his tongue slightly protruding out of his mouth.

PUZU **laughed at Nadin's expression: It's just the way my father drank so, I still do, too! It makes the taste of the beer last longer on the tongue.**

Nadin tried it and nodded, still not quite sure about this method of drinking.

Puzu sipped; Nadin sipped. They went back and forth like this for almost 15 minutes.

PUZU: **Are you still thirsty? Or, did drinking slowly do as well at keeping the tongue wet?**

NADIN: **I can see why you drink slowly. I will have to think on this experience to decide if I like it or not.**

PUZU: **Understood. And I shall have to think about drinking a fast one from time to time.**

PUZU **reached for his empty purse. He rolled it around in his hands and thought about what he and Nadin had just done.**

PUZU: **The problem is … is that now I have used all my coins on drinking games. Fast or Slow. The money is gone. I knew I didn't need another beer, but I wanted to share the experience. I think that in the future, I will decide on which game to play, which game I will let steal my money.**

NADIN: **True. I like my beer, but this is a different way to drink. I may decide one week to drink fast and the next week to drink slow. That way I can change my habits and become a master of them instead of letting them steal from me.**

PUZU: **It was just so easy to spend the money on the beer. It is something I enjoy. But, I can see that I will never get rich if I drink all of my savings.**

Historical Notes:
Ancient Egyptian women perfected the art of brewing beer. They invented the lighter, smoother brew that could be poured into a glass. (Prior to that, beer was dense, put into a glass and water was added.) The average beer likely only had a 3% or 4% alcohol content. It was given to workers three times a day as part of their rations. It was fairly nutritious and, on average, not very intoxicating. Men, women and children all drank the common beer. However, some beers were made to be strong and were used at ceremonies and religious events.

Considering that science had not yet proved that bacteria floating in water caused all kinds of diseases, it is thought that the prolific use of beer actually extended a person's life. Since alcohol can kill bacteria, it made the beer safer to drink than the water.

Generalization:

What's the difference between wants and needs?

Simple: A need is something that you HAVE TO HAVE in order to survive. You must have water, food and shelter. (Though, those who can't afford housing sometimes get by living in a car. The car would serve a dual purpose of shelter and transportation.) A want is something you DESIRE. These differences can be tricky.

If the cheapest food around you is at a fast food Mexican Restaurant on Tuesday night for Taco Night and you don't have much money, Taco Night looks good and it solves the problem of hunger. So, you could NEED food and you LOVE and DESIRE tacos. Depending on a person's situation, there might not be much difference.

Let's join our imaginary friend at the counter as he orders tacos – 3/$1.00. (Normally, they might be $2.00 per taco.) Now – he buys himself two orders of three tacos for $2.00 and decides he wants a BIG drink to take with him. That drink costs another $2.00. Dinner is now $4.00. He stops at ordering extra fries or tortilla chips – because he doesn't think he really NEEDS them. And he leaves off on the ice cream or churro (sweet desserts). He has made some reasonable choices to try to save. His dinner consists of 6 tacos and a drink. That gives him protein in the meat, complex carbohydrates in the taco shell and some simple carbohydrates and liquid in the drink. (Unfortunately, his food is probably loaded with sugar, salt and oils, but let's let him be for now!)

Our friend recognized that he needed food, and tacos were his favorites anyway. It was a win-win for him. He also knew that he didn't really HAVE TO HAVE the fries or the sweets. He made choices to save his money for another meal.

Compare: Another imaginary friend walks into a convenience store. She has only $4.00 and she can buy chips, soda, nachos, hotdogs, water, fruit, candy – whatever. She NEEDS food and liquid. How do you think she SHOULD spend her money to get the nutrition she needs?

It's so easy to walk into a store like that and buy what looks GOOD! But, remember that she needs certain things for her body to keep her well. Her WANTs may not provide the nutrients she needs. Sad, but true.

Let's step back – being reasonable:
You may have a roof over your head, food and water. So – certain categories of things fall into the WANTS. Candies, cakes, cookies, ice cream, chips, oily products, fried products, *overly* bready products. If you already have some good clothes to wear, MORE CLOTHES AND SHOES can be just WANTS. You may have an older car and buying a newer car would be COOL but EXPENSIVE. A newer car may be just a WANT. You may have already gone out on Friday night when another opportunity to spend more money on Saturday night comes up. That extra night out is a WANT. You love trying out new make-up/cosmetics/hair care products. You already have plenty but a new product catches your interest. The new product is a WANT. The list goes on.

IF your objective is to save, you will have to learn to tell yourself "No!" and to recognize when you are rationalizing a purchase. "I could wear that for someone's wedding someday." This one is for "some day" that may never come – and, besides, bridal themes could change the attire! "I bet everyone would notice my new thing/necklace/watch." If you're waiting of "everyone" to notice, perhaps you're WANTing something for the wrong reason. "These new shoes would go perfect with that hard-to-match color!" If that color is already hard to match, then your shoes won't be worn that often and they are simply a WANT. "The guy/gal down the street just bought a new one of these doohickeys and mine looks so drab next to theirs – this will be perfect to shine right next to theirs!" Whatever that thing is, it's supposed to be good for you because you NEED it, not to show up better next to someone else's!!

The character, Kheruef, says that the object you are buying is "stealing your money." In truth, YOU are buying that object and stealing the money from your future self. He says that the thing is stealing from you to help the people understand the concept. Once you understand what self-control is about, you will "get" what stealing from yourself means.

The Characters:

Puzu and Nadin both enjoy drinking beer – just enjoying it differently. They are so enamored of their beer that they undoubtedly will not stop drinking altogether – even if they recognize it as a WANT.

Nadin likes to go on the 3rd day of each week to the same spot to guzzle down beer. If he truly had a need for liquid refreshment, it's highly unlikely that it would show up on exactly the same day at the same time – AND coincide with Aladdin's arrival of freshly made beer. His drinking definitely fulfills a WANT.

Puzu has a more philosophical way of looking at his drinking. He likes to go to enjoy the flavor and the coolness of the Cave. His is probably a WANT but it could be an experience he enjoys and so, beer drinking oddly feeds his soul. If he only goes occasionally, his spending will not get in his way. It is probably still a WANT, but his directive serves as a lesson. He realizes that he will never grow rich if he drinks up all of his savings.

Slowing down to enjoy the experience is one way to service a WANT while not having it become an enslaver of you. Experiences are what make life worth living. So, a WANT that seconds as a fresh experience is probably worth some attention. If the experience is a repeat … like another beer at the same old bar, another smoothie at the same old shoppe, another candy bar at the same old convenience store … it might not be worth the same amount as going with a friend to a trendy bar across town just to try it out. Repetition CAN be fine, but if overdone, it just feeds a WANT.

Some WANTS are fine. Wanting all the time, and serving those wants is dangerous to your savings and possibly fool-hardy when it comes to overspending and not being able to pay the necessary bills that keep you solvent.

The Third Step
Compare Before You Buy

KHERUEF hears his students before he walks in! Their full purses ring loudly.
KHERUEF: **I notice many of you ringing the coins in your purses like they were bells! Very good!**

MANY **laugh!**

KHERUEF: **Can anyone give me some observations about last week's lesson? How did it go for you?**

MARDUK: **The date cakes didn't win <u>every</u> time! *(laughs weakly)***

KHERUEF: **Were you able to win the battle of wills most of the time?**

MARDUK: **Yes. *(thoughtfully)* Most of the time.**

KHERUEF: (looks at crowd and asks all): **Do we have others here who had some trouble fighting back your bad habits?**

MANY in the crown grumble and agree.

KHERUEF: **It will get easier, I promise. All your life, if you had the means, you told yourself "Yes!" when it came to giving to yourself. Now, it will be up to you to gain control over your spending. It will feel like a battle sometimes. And sometimes you will stop the beast from stealing your money. When you win that battle, be sure to put the money away in its safe place, and give yourself something else that doesn't cost money.**

QISHTI: **Like what? Everything costs money!**

KHERUEF: **It seems like that sometimes. You may have to challenge what you value to come up with other things. Can I hear from people here what might be a reward that doesn't cost anything?**

AYA: **Time spent talking with a good friend.**

ELUTIL: **Sleeping in the hammock with my baby at the end of the day.**

NADIN: **If you are going to indulge in your treat, slowing the time it takes to do the task so it feels like you are getting to do it longer. Puzu taught me this when drinking beer. All my life I have guzzled my beer, but he taught me how to slow down and enjoy it. And, now, I know a way to make the fewer times I drink feel like they last longer.**

KHERUEF: **Puzu! You are a wise man! You will have to show me this trick sometime.**

PUZU: **I'd be delighted.**

KHERUEF: **Any other things?**

NAMMU: **I like to fish and hunt but when I don't have time, I will walk on the shore of the Great Nile River and watch others for a while, and it makes me feel happier.**

MARDUK: **When I was a child, just outside of Babylonia, I loved to draw. I think I could do that on clay or on papyrus. I already put some decoration on the shields I make. Perhaps I could think of more.**

ENLIL: **I used to go out on the Great Nile River in a small boat. The gentle waves and the breeze always calmed me. I could do that more.**

KHERUEF: **I hear the long, lost voices of pleasant times past coming back to you. Not everything in life costs money, even if it seems like it! Keep thinking, but we must move on.**
KHERUEF: **Today, we need to talk about comparison shopping. Someday, when you are rich, you will not have to think about what an items costs. But, if you are NOT thinking about this now, you need to start. You cannot live the life of a rich person until you are one!!**

KHERUEF: **Let's start at the market. You should spend some time checking to see what the many bread makers charge. I'll let you in on a little trick. The bread in the center of the market costs less than the bread at the stand right next to the road. Yet, it is still as good. Can you think why the bread by the road costs more?**

ENLIL: **I can say why from experience! If a traveler is in a hurry, and wants a piece of bread before he keeps moving on, he will buy the more expensive bread by the road because he's rushed. The few coins' difference will not matter to him. On the other hand, if my stand is in the middle of the market, not everyone wants to wander that far. So, I make the most delicious breads and entice my customers to come to me. They are rewarded when they come to me by the bread slices being less expensive and slightly bigger. And, the variety never ends! I try new things all the time!**

KHERUEF: Are you, now, still in the middle of the market?

ENLIL: Yes. AND, my customers are very loyal!

KHERUEF: Then, I will have to come by and try your bread!
KHERUEF: Suppose you were buying clothing. Who might be selling clothes for less?

ELUTIL: Now, I can answer. There are several reasons why clothing costs more or less. The cloth that makes the clothing is not always the same. Some cloth is finely woven. Kammani's cloth, though she knows me not, is of exceptional quality! When a seamstress makes clothing with her finely woven linen, it has a divine feel to it. Another example is a young seamstress who has just taken training from an older one, and she may want to try starting a business of her own. She may have good clothing items, but because no one knows her, she must charge less at first. And finally, some items are worn and used up so quickly that they must be replaced often. We see this with children. So, many items of clothing are quickly made and are not meant to last a long, long time. They will cost less.

KHERUEF: Excellent description! I think many of you can see that shopping around might be a way of saving money on things that you truly NEED.
KHERUEF: Here's something those of you who are single might consider. Those with families often already make their own meals. If you are the kind of person who finds yourself eating from a vendor's stand all the time, consider learning to make some of those meals at home. Learn to tend a small fireplace with a cooking rock. Making a flat bread and stuffing it at home is one of the easiest meals and it can be as tasty as one you buy from the market.

KHERUEF: Your assignment is to go to the market and look around, ask questions, but not necessarily to buy. If you have your own business, you also need to compare your product to others'. If you sell your product to someone who then sells it again at the market, like, say, herbs or spices or vegetables, you might want to go see how much they charge compared to what you charged them! Now THERE'S an eye opening experience!!
KHERUEF: Until next week then!

The next day, Ishtar, maker of blades, and Ninkurra, maker of pottery, saw each other at the Market.

ISHTAR: Hello! It's Ninkurra, right?

NINKURRA: **Yes, and you are Ishtar. You speak sometimes about your craft in class. You make blades.**

ISHTAR: **You have a good memory. I must admit that I have forgotten what you make. Tell me again so I might remember.**

NINKURRA: **I make pottery – every day pottery. Cups, plates and bowls.**

ISHTAR: **Right! I remember the joke you made now about how everyone comes to you sooner or later because people break things all the time!!** ***(laughs)***

NINKURRA: **Right you are!** ***(smiles)***

ISHTAR: **Maybe we can help each other out. When we find a stall that has blades, you can ask a few questions to start. And I'll ask questions to begin a conversation at a pottery booth. That way we won't sound like know-it-alls at the beginning – even IF we do "know it all!"**

NINKURRA: **Let's begin our wandering. Let's see how this will work. There's a pottery stall right up here. Let's start by just looking to see what the seller has to offer.**

They walked into an area with stacks of plates and bowls. Ninkurra looked at the top one and removed it to look at the next. It looked much the same, but was chipped. Ishtar walked up to the woman who was selling.

ISHTAR: **Are you the maker of these plates?**

Pottery SELLER 1: **No, my sister stays at home and makes these.**

ISHTAR: **How much do the plates in this stack sell for?**

SELLER 1: **The chipped ones sell for two coins. The best ones sell for five coins.**

NINKURRA: **Why do you sell the chipped ones?**

The seller looked in her direction.
SELLER: **Some of the plates chip by the time we get them here. And there are poor people who still need a plate and yet, they can't afford the best ones. Some chips are on the back sides of the plates, so they <u>look</u> fine. And the poor are pleased to find those.**

ISHTAR: **Do you have a price difference for every item here? Like … the cups and bowls?**

SELLER 1: **The cups vary by size. Small cups are one coin for chipped and three coins for the best cups. The large cups sell for the same as the plates. The bowls are all different. From small to very large. They can be anywhere from three to seven coins.**

NINKURRA: **You have a very clever pricing system! Thank-you for explaining this to us.**

Ninkurra smiled at Ishtar and they left.

NINKURRA: **I noticed that she has very simple plates - no designs. But, she had a wide variety of bowl sizes! And, she still manages to sell the chipped ones. I often break my damaged plates apart and remix them with water to use the clay over again. Still, I can see that she sells the chipped ones as a service to the poor.**

ISHTAR: **Yes! I liked that she did that, too. I could do something similar. When I break the rocks, they do not always break the same way … or the right way! Yet, there are often small, but very sharp blades. That was very informative. Let's move down this way. I see a blade seller.**

They walked down a short alley to a small booth where a man sat on the ground with a sheet of cow's hide over his lap. He used a large rock to break apart the blade rock. Even as he sold his blades, he made more.

NINKURRA: **Good morning to you! You are so busy! Do you make, as well as sell, the blades or do you have a helper?**

The blade SELLER 2 looked up and saw the two of them. Instead of speaking to Ninkurra, he spoke instead to Ishtar.

SELLER 2: **I do both. I have no help. What can I do for you?**

Ishtar looked at Ninkurra.
ISHTAR: **Good woman, what did you see that you'd like to ask about?**

Ninkurra turned her back to the Seller and smiled broadly at Ishtar, as if to laugh. Ishtar kept his face calm as he looked back at the Seller. Ninkurra put on her solemn face and turned back around to look at the blades with handles.

NINKURRA: **The blade I use for scoring my clay has recently dulled. Its sharp blade was good for designs. I need to replace it with a handled blade. What about this blade here? How much is it, as well as the ones slightly smaller and slightly larger?**

The Blade SELLER 2 glanced at the blades she mentioned and continued to talk to Ishtar.

SELLER 2: **The blades the woman mentions are between seven and fifteen coins. And, you sir. What kind of blade would you like to see? I have many large, versatile blades. Manly blades for carving meat and cedar.**

Ishtar glanced around realizing that the man wanted to make the biggest sale he could instead of small, fine blades and on seeing a large hand blade asked about it.

ISHTAR: **Of course. How much is this blade, and do you have any larger?**

The Seller beamed.
SELLER 2: **The one you see is 25 coins. I have one larger for 30 coins. I could bring it tomorrow. You have a good eye for quality.**

ISHTAR: **Yes. Thank you. I won't need anything larger. Thank you for showing me your fine work. I will go back to my employer and ask about getting the coins to buy such a blade. If he consents, I will come back.**

The Seller looked deflated.

ISHTAR: **I'd like to make a suggestion. You should move your booth closer to the road so that people coming by can see you more easily. I just happened to see you, but we had to walk down this alley to get to you. I believe you could make more sales by being closer to the foot traffic.**

The Seller nodded thoughtfully. Ninkurra and Ishtar walked back down the alley and further into the market.

NINKURRA: **You are so smart! I thought at first that he was just being rude to me. But, clearly, he wanted to make a sale badly. And, you shared what we had learned in class. You were so kind to that man. I hope he takes your words to heart.**

ISHTAR: **I, too, still have days when I make no sales. But, Ninkurra, he WAS rude to you, even if I understand why. He could have had a little money if he'd worked harder at your sale. Instead, because we came together, he assumed I would want a more manly and, therefore, larger blade. I learned a lot from this man by watching how he tried to make a sale. What TO DO and what NOT TO DO.**

NINKURRA: **I am glad we are walking this market together. Let's see what else we learn today.**

Ninkurra and Ishtar spent a few hours walking around the market, each making excuses about why they would not be able to buy anything today. Before they parted ways, they each purchased a small flat bread stuffed with chickpeas, cucumbers, and yogurt. The chatted over lunch about what they had seen and what they had learned.

NINKURRA: **I saw designs I hadn't seen in pottery before that makes the plates and bowls just a little more expensive than mine. I think I could incorporate some of that into a more expensive line of plates. What about you?**

ISHTAR: **I noticed that some of the handles on the blades had designs in them and some handles were shaped differently. I thought that was innovative. Though I don't know how to carve, I could probably learn. Like you, I'm thinking I could have inexpensive items and more expensive items to appeal to a broader range of people.**

NINKURRA: **It was good to see you here. I'm glad we explored together. You have a good way of clarifying your thoughts. It helped me see things in a new way.**

ISHTAR: **And, I liked your attention to detail. You saw things that I didn't see. This was a good market trip for both of us.**

Historical Notes:
Poor and middle class people ate from earthenware plates and bowls. The rich had bowls of gold, silver, and wood (which was scarce), like African imported ebony. The variety of metal plates often had carvings in them, such as archery matches or chariot races.

Throughout ancient Egyptian history, the flint knife was popular owing to the ease of finding, or trading, for flint/chert. Later, copper knives were made, but they never matched the sharpness of flint. Both flint and copper knives broke easily in combat.

Generalization:

Why comparison shop?

Simple: True story. Check it out yourselves. A (real) Barbie doll in a discount store could cost you $7.00. That exact same Barbie could cost you 3 times that much, or $21.00, if sold in a boutique in Hollywood. If you're buying a present for a little friend/cousin/sibling of yours, will that child even notice the one bought at a discount store? Wrapped up, they all look the same.

Economics:
Try this one on for size. Generally, gasoline that's sold at a freeway exit or near an on-ramp costs more than gas sold further into the city. How can this be? The difference is known as "what the market will bear." If an item is priced too high, the people (the market) won't purchase it. If an item is sold too low, everyone might buy it, but you won't make any money/profit as a merchant. So, the seller must figure out how to set the price at just the right spot so that the market (the people) will be able to bear (tolerate) the price. This difference in cost is also known and "The Price of Convenience."

When Kheruef talks about the bread seller who is next to the roadway selling bread for more than the person close to the center of the market, he knows whereof he speaks! A person who just wants to fill the gas tank of the car and jump back on the freeway is willing to spend the extra money so that he/she isn't wasting time. If you're willing to travel a bit farther, you could probably find cheaper gas ... but are you willing to spend the time doing that? And if the city is new to you, are you willing to "get lost" just for cheaper gas?

Making it work – the practicality of it all:
Grocery stores play this same game. If you're buying a can of Whole Peeled Tomatoes to make your famous spaghetti sauce, a "warehouse" grocery store will often have the exact same can as a convenience store or a specialty shop where the same can will cost more. If people with more money shop the trendy stores, most of the prices will be more expensive.

Another place to find discounts is at outlet stores. Nike shoes at a specialty shop will cost more than if you're willing to shop at their outlet stores.

While we're at it ... if you're willing to wear cute knock-offs or lookalikes, you might not have to wear what the rest of the world is wearing. And, by not competing, you can free yourself from the one-upmanship.

The truth is ... is that we pay for convenience. (It's closer , I already know the store layout, I don't have to search to find what I want, It's RIGHT HERE.) If you can "inconvenience" yourself, you may find you spend less money for the same items.

The characters: Ninkurra and Ishtar find out more than just the cost of items. They see that sellers vary in the way they present items, talk to customers, make deals, etc. Since they themselves are business people, they learn things that they could do better or differently. They learn as they go along.

You could do well to learn as you go along, too. Watch to see how the people in line purchase items. Do they seem to have been working from a list? In other words, were they mindfully shopping so as not to purchase more than they needed? Did they clip coupons or belong to the store's "loyalty" shopping group (often an App or a code to enter on purchasing)? There should be no embarrassment in purchasing the same item for less money!!

The Fourth Step
Invest in Yourself

KHERUEF walked into the room to see general talking.
KHERUEF: **Can someone ask a question about last week's assignment? Or offer an observation?**

NINKURRA: **I ran into Ishtar at the Market and we wandered around for several hours talking to many like-minded businesses. What I noticed was that the craftsmanship was either a bit lower than my own or equal to my own for what I make. However, many people had different methods of selling and there were as many ways to sell an item as there are people selling! Some were loud, some were quiet, some followed us down the aisle even after we had left their stall! *(laughs)***

KHERUEF: **It's true! But didn't that diversity make the walk all that much more interesting? Imagine if every vendor yelled at you or every vendor was quiet!**

NINKURRA: **I hadn't thought of it that way, but yes! It was fun partly because it was unpredictable. However, I have a question. At one of the stands, a woman sold good and chipped pottery. The chipped plates she would sell to poor customers and the best plates went to those who could afford it. Is this a good idea? Or would selling damaged goods in your stall be off-putting to the richer clients?**

KHERUEF: **Good question! The person selling the chipped pottery to the poor made a choice based on her values. If you care about making your product available to everyone, then you could do the same. If it isn't important to you, no one will be the wiser – except for the poor who won't come to see what you've got. As for your other customers, who knows what they will think? Like-minded people will come to see you as a good person. If it is upsetting to another, then they won't buy. What you sell, in that case, and how you sell it will be a representation of who you are and what you believe. What did you think when you saw it?**

ISHTAR: **May I speak? We talked about it and generally agreed that we both liked the idea. It made me realize that sometimes my "mistakes" as I make tools could be useful to someone else. And, the small amount of coins it would cost would make items available to those who can't have the more expensive item. We felt that everyone should have a chance to own something of worth.**

KHERUEF: **Is there anyone who can see this a different way?**

QISHTI: **I would never show second class work to one of my clients! It would be a disgrace! I wouldn't want them to know that I even PRODUCE products of poor quality…which I don't!**

KHERUEF: **Thank you! Clearly, Qishti, your clientele expects to see a high quality product. And, don't you see individuals? And not spend time in a stall in the Market?**

QISHTI: **I only go to the market to shop for food for my table. Most of my clients send their slaves to get their food, so they would never even go to a Market. Period.**

KHERUEF: **So, class, if I were you and I was selling in the Market Place where most people go, I would sell to everyone and anyone. And I would be kind to whoever walked up to buy something from me, large or small purchases.**

KHERUEF: **Let's move on. I will not talk of coins or gold today. Instead I will talk about you, the ones who sit before me. In your lives, there are ways to act that can work either for or against your success. Desiring to be rich is good, but you must have the skill to back it up. Therefore, you must make of yourselves, the best that you can be in your chosen areas. You must invest in yourself. If you are creating something for ten coins but another across town is producing a better product and selling it for less, you cannot hope to compete. You must learn all that you can learn about what you do, and then do MORE than your competition, work HARDER than your competition and SURPASS your competition. Only in this way will you be WORTH more than your competition.**

If you are working FOR someone, watch to see what others do and then, do it better. Do not look around to see if you are being watched and only work hard when you know someone is near. No … you need to work hard ALL the time to prove your worth, so that when you ask for a raise from your employer, there will be no question about it. As you perfect yourself and your abilities, so do you increase your ability to earn.

DELONDRA : **How am I to do that if I don't know anyone?**

KHERUEF: **Are you aware of others who do the same thing as you?**

DELONDRA: **Yes, but we do not speak.**

KHERUEF: **Then, you must start the conversation! Go to this person and introduce yourself. Speak knowledgably of your profession, but do not brag. See what this person knows and spend time watching another as they work.**

ELUTIL: **How can I spend time THERE when I am needed at my own workshop?**

KHERUEF: **How is it that you are able to be here with me today?**

ELUTIL: **I wanted to know how to become rich! This is important to me!**

KHERUEF: **If being rich is important, then your own training should be as important to you. Watch, discover, learn, teach yourself, train yourself with what you have seen. Improve on what you find out. You must invest time in your own education.**

LUGAL indignantly: **You're telling us to work harder than all those around us!**

KHERUEF: **How will you stand out if you act and look like everyone around you? How will you attract the attentions of your employer or of your customers if you look and act like everyone else? You must find your inner strength to push yourself to do better and then demonstrate to others your cleverness and expertise. You must rise above your competition to become worthy of recognition.**

LUGAL: **But!**

KHERUEF cuts him off: **We have all seen the races. The foot races and the chariot races. The trained racer who wins does so because he has trained for the distance <u>and more</u>. He has not run 100 yards once a day if he is to win a race that is 100 yards long. He trains by running 300, 400, maybe 500 yards a day, perhaps longer distances, getting faster and stronger. The chariot driver practices in all kinds of weather, in good and poor conditions so that his animals might build resistance to unseemly circumstances. If they all trained the same, the outcome would not be as outstanding as watching the finely trained athlete cross the finish line far ahead of his competition.**

KHERUEF looks at them all quite seriously: **<u>You</u> must be the one to cross the finish line first! So to speak. Do not be happy with making products that are almost good. Be only happy producing excellent products that stand out as valued treasures.**

KHERUEF smiles at the group: **Know this, my friends. Exceptional products will bring you more gold.**

KHERUEF: **Your assignment is to spend time meeting those whose professions are like yours and to start a conversation about how you both accomplish the same or similar tasks.**

As they left, Taram, chicken, duck and geese raiser, caught up with Delondra, cow milker.

TARAM: **Wait! I have an idea!**

DELONDRA: (speaks sarcastically) **Oh, it's you. The egg in the basket woman.**

TARAM: (laughs uproariously) **HAHAHA! You are sooo funny!**

DELONDRA: **What? What did I do now?**

TARAM: **Okay. Look at me. Do I look like anyone you know?**

DELONDRA: **No. So what?**

TARAM: **Have I ever done anything to harm you, make you mad, or be mean to you?**

DELONDRA: **No.**

TARAM: **Here's what I'm going to do. Let's start over. I'm going to pretend that we've just met and you're going to pretend the same. Let's try this again.**
TARAM: (deep breath) **Hi! Wait! I have an idea!!**

DELONDRA: **Hi. What ... *(sigh)* ... idea do you have?**

TARAM: **Better!**
TARAM**: I know some people who own farms with lots of different animals. I have a donkey and it can hold us both. I think you and I should take a ride out to the country and see what they do that's different from what we do.**

DELONDRA: **You'd take me on your donkey? Why?**

TARAM: **We both work with farm animals and the Market isn't the place to find out how people do things differently. I can pick you up.**

DELONDRA: **Um. Okay. Tell me when and where and I can go. How long will we be gone?**

TARAM: **Probably most of the morning.**

Taram and Delondra arranged for a meeting three days later. Once Delondra got settled on the donkey and was convinced she wouldn't fall off, the two of them left for their ride out to the farms.

The first stop was at a farm at the edge of the town. Geese, chickens, donkeys, cows and goats all shared several pastures. The farmer tending them came out and recognized Taram directly.

FARMER: **Taram! Jump down and come see me. It has been many suns since I've seen you! How is your father? Is he still as crazy as always?**

TARAM: **Uncle! How good to see you! This is my new friend, Delondra. She milks cows and sells the milk. Can we talk as we go about the farm?**

FARMER: **Of course. I was just about to go out to the shed to see about milking the cows. Look! They're all running to get in line. Have you ever milked a cow this size? No? Well, come watch and learn!**

Taram spoke about her father as her Uncle went on about his farm and never finding enough good help. He pulled up a small stool and put a crock under the udder. As each cow passed him, he whispered something sweet in its ear and stroked it between the eyes. Sometimes he kissed it gently on the forehead. He thanked each cow for the milk it was going to give. As he milked the cows, he saw Delondra watching intently.

FARMER: **Here, Delondra. Come milk the next animal. Her name is Sweet One. Pet her ears first so she knows you'll be gentle.**

Delondra did as the Farmer had done, and soon the Sweet One had filled the crock. Delondra smiled. The Farmer scooped up a dipper full and let Delondra drink the fresh milk.

DELONDRA: **It is sweet! This is delicious!**

FARMER: **The secret is in the grass I let them graze on. Every other day, I let them into the field with the alfalfa. Then on the other days, I give them their regular feed. People come to buy my milk from all over!**

Delondra smiled.

TARAM: **Come Delondra, we need to move on down the road.**

FARMER: **If your trip brings you back this way, stop to have lunch with me!**

TARAM: **Uncle, we'd be delighted. We have to come back this way anyway. See you soon.**

The women got back on the donkey and headed out to another farm. At the first farm, no one was home, so they stood outside the pastures and watched the animals. On this farm, there was a small pond that all of the animals shared and Taram noted that the ducks and geese were especially happy to have a place to paddle around. She

also pointed out a slanted shelter that a few cows were standing under to get out of the sun. Delondra nodded.

At the next farm, a woman was at home with the children. Taram introduced them and what they were looking to find out.

WOMAN: **You're just in time! My girls are out back playing with the ducks.**

TARAM: **Playing? With the ducks? Why?**

WOMAN: **We discovered a few years ago when my oldest daughter, who's now 6, started playing with the ducklings. As they grew up together, instead of biting at her hand as she fed them, they came and waited patiently or took the food without biting her. The ducks are quite friendly when we help them get used to us when they're young. Come watch.**

Three girls, the oldest – 6, and two more, one 4 and one 2, sat on the yard handling the ducklings. They cuddled and kissed them and the 2 year old sang baby songs to them. The ducklings were calm and happy to be held.

TARAM: **Can I try? I have never handled my ducks very much. This might make a huge difference in my job!**

Taram sat next to the oldest and the girl taught her how to hold the duckling and what the duck seemed to like most. Taram felt like a kid again, nuzzling the soft down of the babies. Delondra joined them after watching a while and even she couldn't resist the ducklings' softness.

TARAM: **Thank-you for letting us join your daughters. So, you come out here once a day? Or more?**

WOMAN: (laughing) **It's hard to keep the girls away. And, if they're underfoot in the house, I send them out here! So, they come out here 3 or 4 times a day. Even the older ducks who've been raised by the girls come around. It gets noisy but they are all part of the family now! Here come some of the older ones.**
WOMAN: **Girls! Get some food and show us all how good the ducks are.**

The girls grabbed handfuls of grain and waited until the larger ducks were around. The ducks seemed to have their favorite child and honked and quacked at them. When they threw down the food, the ducks pecked greedily. One of the girls called her favorite duck to her and the duck ate gently from her hand.

TARAM: **This is amazing. I'm so glad I came on this trip today. I've learned so much! Thank you, good woman. Thank you.**

Taram and Delondra rode back the way they had come and stopped back at Taram's uncle's house.

TARAM: **Uncle! We're back. Hello!**

FARMER: **Come sit in the cow shed! It's cooler here and I have lunch waiting.**

TARAM: **It's nice in here. Won't the cows kick you out?**

FARMER: **We've been known to share this space, but I love all of my cows so much that we know how to get along!!**
FARMER: **So, Delondra. What did you learn about today?**

DELONDRA: **I learned that if you start being very kind and friendly to the animals when they are quite young, they will remain friendly with you all their lives.**

TARAM: **I've always known about you and your dairy cows, but a woman down the way has her children play with the ducklings and the birds grow up to be quite gentle!**

FARMER: **I haven't seen that with ducks, but you say this is so?**
TARAM: **I saw it with my own eyes! And I handled some of the babies. They were so soft!**

FARMER: **Good! It sounds like you had a good day. Now, let's eat so you can get back home before the heat is unbearable!**

Temperatures in Karnak ranged from a low of 76 degrees Fahrenheit in January to 110 in mid-summer. Many slept during the day and were active in early morning, early evening and at night. As previously mentioned, they had ways of making smaller environs cooler using evaporative cooling techniques, but that can only be useful so far.

Generalization:

The truth is, you will need to go and find training where it is most logical for you to learn. If you are trying to learn a trade, you will need to go to a trade school and apprentice with a master at the craft – say, construction, or plumbing. If you want to work with farm animals, you'll need to go to a farm or a veterinary college. If you want to learn about coding or website designing, you might go to a trade school, or you could watch "how to videos" on your favorite site. Whatever it is, you must commit to learning as much as you can. If you don't stand out in the crowd, how will people know to hire you?

Beware of becoming arrogant:
When some people get good at doing something, they begin to feel that no one can do it better than they can. Be careful because if you are one of those kinds of people, you will inadvertently put others down. That unawareness of the struggle others go through, or the strides they are taking to become better (or just like you) belittles them and makes them feel awkward around you, or they end up just not liking to be near you. Bragging, being overly proud, being overly self-important and self-absorbed, and ignoring the work that others are doing in your same field will make you unpopular (not that you have to care a LOT about that if you are specializing) and undesired. The problem then becomes in finding someone who will hire you or take you on when your ego is so inflated. If you're just seeing what the competition is like, do it carefully and, perhaps, judiciously.

Lessons Learned:
- By watching others, sometimes you will learn WHAT to do and at other times you will learn WHAT NOT to do.
- Variation on a theme (pattern, way of doing things) is what makes the world interesting.
- Good Work Habits (as well as Bad Work Habits) can be contagious. Choose wisely. I once worked at a place where the only time my co-worker worked was when the boss came in the room. More than once, when I wasn't there, she took responsibility for what I'd done.

The characters:
Delondra actually suffers from low self-esteem. It can LOOK like she thinks she's all that by her initial actions toward Taram. Taram is lucky in that she doesn't seem to have those issues. She recognizes that some of Delondra's bluster is just because she isn't quite as sure about her job as she could be. (She doesn't talk to anyone in her line of work.) If you come up against someone like her, or like the kind of person described before that, have a bit of a sense of humor. They aren't behaving that way because of anything *you* did, but because of the world *they* live in. Know who you are and be tolerant of those who have not had your opportunities to grow up.

The Half Step
Keep Safe and Guard Your Wealth

KHERUEF strides in purposefully.
KHERUEF: **I had not thought that I would make this part of my talk, but every time I walk in here, I hear you jingling your purses. So, without any discussion, we will now talk about keeping safe and guarding your wealth.**

KHERUEF: **When you show off your wealth – by jingling your purse, by wearing expensive jewelry, by dressing in very fine clothes all just to go shopping at the Market – you open yourself up to unseemly characters. Some will be crude and just take your money purse and run. Others will threaten and beat you up – or worse – kill you if they think you are worth it. If you are simply masquerading – dressing and walking as IF you are a rich person – then the thieves will be very angry with you indeed and may not show mercy.**

KHERUEF: **From here on out, you will carry your purses in a normal fashion… either tied around your waist or hidden in a fold of your garment. If you need to, put a cloth IN the purse to help deaden the noise of the coins. When you go into the market, do NOT put all of your money out so that the vendor can see it. You never know who is watching you or from where. Learn to feel the coins in their hiding place and to pull out approximately the correct amount.**

KHERUEF: **Do NOT talk to strangers and tell them where you live. Don't even tell them "somewhere over there" and point – ESPECIALLY, if, in fact, you will be walking that direction when you leave the market. Thieves often work together and they may try to ambush you on your way home – away from the crowds at the Market.**

KHERUEF: **If you frequent the Market, be wary of the thief who is willing to work for a long time to gain your trust. These are the hardest to figure out. You will see them sometimes, but not all of the time. They will have open conversations with you and they will share with you information that SOUNDS like it could be true. You will end up having a lot in common. In the end, they will gain your trust and you will lose your money. If you think someone may be doing that, ask the vendors if they see this person talking to others openly and sharing. Find out if you can trust this curious person who wants to know so much about you.**

KHERUEF: **We are so interested in sharing. We think when someone shows an interest, that they truly are interested. We think, "I'm flattered that this person finds**

me interesting!" It boosts your sense of worth. But be wary of too much attention put on you.

KHERUEF: **I'm not saying that you shouldn't be friendly with people there in the market. It's a big world and there are many interesting people here. But, do not share your most intimate and important details. Speak of the last celebration to the gods, the last flood that graced us with such rich soil, or a booth in the market that you found interesting. Steer clear of conversations about where you live, how much money you make, how much money you carry with you, who you live with, and members of your family. You MUST be careful!**

KHERUEF: **As for the money that you're saving at home. Make sure that your young children do NOT know where you hide the money until they come of age. Children love to get into things that they shouldn't have and they talk about private things with anyone when you wish they would not! Consider digging a hole in a closet or under a low table and putting a crock in the hole that can be sealed. Then cover the hole so that it looks normal. Perhaps even put a small rug over an area where you sit covering your crock, so you'll know it is directly below you as you rest at the end of the day. The fewer who know where your jar is, the better. I once heard of a house that had burned down. Upon returning to the structure, the man who lived there went directly to where his crock should be and dug it up. He had saved enough to help him and his family resettle. You can do this, too.**

KHERUEF: **It may seem that I am not who you thought I was by being so brusque today, but I learned yesterday that Belessunu, who makes jewelry for Ptolemy's family, was robbed. When I asked after the circumstances, she had emptied the contents of her purse at a goldsmith's stall. Several people watched as she bargained – with her money in plain sight – and they followed her when she left. She was ambushed and all her gold and coins were stolen. She was shaken and she will be alright. I have been to see her. She will have to start over. But, she learned the hard way not to trust everyone. I want the rest of you to learn from her example.**

KHERUEF: **Your job for this next week is to practice discretion in who you talk to, to carry your coins as if you'd like to keep them, and to make a special place to store your coins at home. We will have a regular class next week.**

Generalization:

If you are on social media, hopefully someone has already had a talk with you about what you can and cannot share. As with the story, don't share personal information such as: income, actual place of your job, the times you go to work and when you get back home, and whether the people you live with are home or gone. If you haven't thought about the consequences of having a public presence consider not sharing things like: pictures of when you or your friends got really drunk or stoned, pictures someone shared with you showing nudity or profanity, videos of you and your buddies breaking the law, videos of fights – staged or otherwise, violence, rape, or other harmful activities. If you post things about other people, you can be held liable for any actions taken against them. What goes around comes around and if you play the game, expect to pay the price.

Money and Plastic:
Don't share your credit or debit cards with anyone. ANYONE. Don't give your passwords or pin numbers to ANYONE. When entering your pin number at a remote teller, be sure to cover your hand so no one can see the actual numbers you touch. (Don't be fooled by the semi-covering provided! It's still possible to watch someone and figure out what numbers you're touching!) Change your passwords every month or so. Keep track of passwords and pin numbers in "lockable", secure files or apps. If your debit or credit card is also a bank card, sign up for alerts when purchases made on your card is larger than, say, $100.00. When I go on vacation, I set that down to $50.00. If I've made the purchase, I recognize it. If I don't recognize it, I can call the bank or check online.

If you still carry money, keep it on your person – in a wallet or in a pocket. Don't carry large bills. If you're heading to a flea market, swap meet or whatever, and you plan on paying cash (probably safer if you know how to handle cash), put your money in several different pockets. That way, if you're bargaining for something, you won't be pulling out ALL of your money and showing the vendor that you actually have MORE than you "sounded" like you did. (Cargo pants with lots of pockets are great for this kind of trip.)

Extra careful:
Going shopping in a high rent district? Dress up but not TOO up. Going to a swap meet or a garage sale? Dress down. Try not to stick out like a sore thumb. Think about the Hollywood actors and actresses who want to shop like normal people at Big Box stores like Costco. They dress down and wear sunglasses and hats. Just saying.

Beware of the on-line presence of someone you are unfamiliar with who is a follower or who has "friended" you. They may have read all of your past entries and figured out your strengths and weaknesses and your likes and dislikes. Using this information, they can "become your best friend." Many swindlers spend years cultivating these friendships so that they can ultimately prey on their target person.

Watch out for a roller coaster ride of emotions as they play to your better self. Something a little sad, followed by something happier, followed by something to make you angry at the world (that you share), followed by something happier. Up-down-Up-down. This keeps you involved in their world and lets you buy into them – because they seem so real. Cultivate a good sense of self and don't let flattery or compliments or over-the-top defense of your side make you think this person truly has your best interests at heart. Remember: a really good friend will tell you when you're wrong, and if this person NEVER thinks you're wrong, think twice about believing in this person 100%. Never go to meet someone for a first time without your normal friends as back up. Then, try to listen to your friends' reactions to this stranger. Are they as taken by the person? Or were they creeped out by his/her fawning over you? Try hard to see it from your friends' perspectives. Use your Spidey Sense!

The Fifth Step
Create a Budget

KHERUEF: **I trust that you have secured your money now. I will not ask you what you have done, as I do not want to know your secrets.**
KHERUEF: **Two weeks ago I sent you out to see what others like you were doing and making. Are there any questions or observations?**

ELUTIL: **I went shopping at a market I don't usually go to and I found many exciting new styles. And, I made friends! I thought other dress makers would be more close-minded, but they were happy to share a few trade secrets. I can use the new ideas in my clothing.**

KHERUEF: **Good! So, your own work will evolve and become even better and more eye-catching. Perhaps they will come see you someday and realize they have fallen behind. Then, the quality will go up where they are again. It is ever so!**

LUGAL: **I understand that! I went to another town closer to where the Pharaoh Ptolemy lives to see what the Scribes were doing. Their work was much harder and more demanding than mine. Clearly, being nearer to the God On Earth requires more exertion and labor. I'm afraid I've gotten lazy!!**

KHERUEF: **(laughs!) I recall going to help one of the pharaoh's Scribe Schools and discovered, I, too, had forgotten what it was like to be a student and how hard we all had to work. So, now you have a choice! Do you work harder to move up to be nearer to the pharaoh? Or, do you stay here to work with the people you know?**

LUGAL: **I believe I want to do something in the middle. I want to work harder and more carefully for the people here. This is my home.**

KHERUEF: **It is a wise man who knows himself.**

TARAM: **I discovered that I had been doing something wrong all my life! I watched young children teach their ducks and geese to be gentle, just by handling them when they were chicks and joining them outside. They played with them almost all of their lives!**

KHERUEF: **I have never heard of such a thing! I remember as a child getting nipped by a goose and it was quite painful!!**

TARAM: **I would not have believed it either if I hadn't seen it.**

DELONDRA: **I saw it too! And then, we saw a farmer who whispers caring, gentle sentiments to his cows and they gave sweet, delicious milk without complaint! They had been raised since babes with calm caresses and spoken language.**

KHERUEF: **It sounds as if the two of you will work this magic with your own animals now! And, we shall all benefit from your attention to these details.**

KHERUEF: **Let's move on.**
KHERUEF: **We must step back to pick up what was to be the original 5th step – creating a budget. You have learned how to put aside one in ten coins, you have thought about what you need versus what you want, you have considered ways to control you expenditures by comparison shopping and you have learned that you should better yourself by learning more about your craft and becoming the best that you can be. Now, we will go into one of the longest classes. That of making a budget and staying the course.**

KHERUEF: **The very first thing you must decide is where you want to take your life. What do you hope to accomplish in this lifetime? Do you want to be fabulously wealthy and move into a rich home with rich neighbors? Or, do you want a comfortable home for your family without needing the trappings of the rich and famous? Do you want to have time to travel? Do you want to be well known for your craft and to have customers waiting to see you at the market every day? Or, would you simply be happy making it to the end of your life while having enough each day and never having to worry about having enough coins? Everyone's goals will be different. And, I don't expect you to make a final judgment right now but I DO need you to think about this BY YOURSELF for just a few moments.**

KHERUEF: **Start thinking now on your own.**

Kheruef came down from his normal speaking podium and wandered among his students. He shushed a few from talking and paused here and there to ensure that all were doing the task at hand.

When he started back up to his platform, he spoke.
KHERUEF: **Can someone tell me why I had you consider this on your own?**

NINKURRA: **I believe you want us to understand WHY we all want to save our money.**

KHERUEF: **And? Anything else?**

BELESSUNU: **To make sure that we buy into the notion of self-discipline as a way to achieve our goals.**

KHERUEF: **Men? Can you add anything here?**

QISHTI: (softly) **So we can understand how far we must go, and how much we must save, before we have reached our goals.**

KHERUEF: (smiles) **And? Any other men?**

ENLIL: **So we may speak of this with our partners when we get home and make a decision together.**

KHERUEF: **All of these things are correct! You see, while you may decide on a goal now, your family and partners may not feel the same. And, the goal you set today, may not be the best goal 10 years down the road. But the only way you will ever move forward is by understanding WHY you want to save and HOW you can make that happen.**

KHERUEF: **Some of you value having a safe and desirable place for your families. Others of you have no family and want to travel the world. Both are fine goals. But only you know what YOU PERSONALLY value most in life. And, that is why you had to think of this on your own. I would not have you influenced by someone who has different values on this important task.**

KHERUEF: **That said, know this. Your values and goals move you forward on your budget. I cannot tell you exactly how to do it, but I will guide your path.**

KHERUEF: **Each of you will need to figure out how much you make. I'll give you my timeline when I first started. As a scribe, I was paid at the end of every week. One week I might earn a little, and the next week I might earn a lot. In order to set my budget, I looked at a four week period. I added all of my income for the four weeks so that a good week didn't make my budget feel I could save hundreds of coins or a bad week didn't make me feel like I could barely save any coins at all.**

ELUTIL: **I understand that! Sometimes, I am paid for some clothing I've made for the pharaoh's daughters and then again, I don't make money for a couple of days. Then, I'll be able to sell some dresses at the Market. Should I add up the days to make four weeks, too?**

KHERUEF: **Yes! Day to day, you will decide what to save and what to pay, but you will have a better idea over all if you use that longer time.**
KHERUEF: **While you are figuring that out, decide what you MUST pay. If you are paying for your house, or renting a room, that will usually stay the same. If you are renting property to grow your crops, it's the same. Figure out how much you spend on home and property for four weeks.**

KHERUEF: We all must eat. Figure out how much you spend in four weeks' time for the food you MUST have. Do not include your date cakes, pomegranates, the extra slice of bread, and the extra beer!

SOME in the class groan. _Others_ laugh.

KHERUEF: Add the home and property fees to the food cost. Those are called Fixed Expenses. You must eat and you must live somewhere. If you are paying for someone else's food, include that. I wouldn't want your aging father or mother to go hungry!

SOME nod.

KHERUEF: Add on some more money for taxes, add the one in ten coins you are saving, and you'll have the bare minimum that you must HAVE TO HAVE.

KHERUEF: Some of you business people can see where I am going.

NAMMU: I think I have it figured out. If we know how much we make, we subtract the amount we MUST SPEND on food and housing and our savings. The rest that is left to us is for …
Nammu looked back at Kheruef for the right words.

KHERUEF: Right! For everything else. If you need clothing, extra food, entertainment costs, OR, you just want to save more. You could parse that last amount into 4 piles and use only that fourth on choice spending for each of the weeks in your budget.

QISHTI: I don't like the idea of a budget! I don't want to be a slave to it! I believe it is my right to enjoy the good things in life! You are suggesting I rob the pleasure from my life!

KHERUEF calmly: Who, my friend, would determine what your budget would be?

QISHTI: (pauses and thinks) I would make it for myself!

KHERUEF: Then, don't make a budget that enslaves you! But carefully consider those casual desires compared to your most cherished desires. Like a bright light in a dark cave, your budget can show you the leaks from your purse and help you to stop them and control them for the important and the clearly significant expenses.

BELESSUNU walked up to Kheruef at the end of the lesson.
BELESSUNU: **I wanted to thank you again for your kind counsel after last week. I was such a fool! I see now that I did almost everything wrong.**

KHERUEF: **You're quite welcome. So, will you also have to start over as I once did?**

BELESSUNU: **Yes. And that's what I wanted to talk to you about as it relates to budgeting.**

They stood and discussed her circumstances briefly and Kheruef gave her advice. Belessunu hurried off, nodding confidently to herself.

Later in the week, Belessunu went to the market. She skipped the stalls and vendors nearest the streets and wandered further into the market. Many people, it seemed, knew that the costs would be less for the market got busier the further into it she walked.

She got distracted by some lovely dresses in one stall and stood outside to admire. She had already decided she would neither touch the cloth nor go in for a visit.

ELUTIL: **Belessunu! Is that you! Come in!**

BELESSUNU: **Oh no! Hello, I mean! I can't come in, for I cannot buy anything today.**

ELUTIL: **I'm just happy to see you. Come! I promise I won't try to sell you anything.**

BELESSUNU: **Your dresses sell themselves! They're beautiful.**

ELUTIL: (laughing) **Come back here, the back of the stall isn't near as interesting as the front. Let me boil some water for some tea.**
ELUTIL: **Have a seat here. One is for my sister who is off running errands. Let's talk.**

They sat next to a very low table, sipping tea and chatting. When the conversation turned to the class, Belessunu relaxed a bit, knowing that focusing on her goals would make the stay easier.

ELUTIL: **And, what do you think of what we're learning?**

BELESSUNU: **I am enjoying it very much. In fact, now that I know more about starting over and budgeting, I think I shall enjoy the process more!**

ELUTIL: **Tell me more.**

BELESSUNU: **Well, I don't have much money left that I had saved. I lost it being foolish at the goldsmith's stall. I will not make that mistake again!**

ELUTIL: **We heard a little of what happened. Tell me again.**

Belessunu told her story and Elutil gasped and sighed and nodded in all the right places. At the end of the story all was quiet for a while.

ELUTIL: (shakes her head) **So, you must start over. What a trial! How do you plan on budgeting with very little money?**

BELESSUNU: **I thought the same. At the end of last class, I talked with Kheruef and do you remember how he taught us to parse the money into 4 sections and give ourselves a week's worth? Well, since I can't do that, he suggested that after everything I earn, on any given day, I put away my one in ten. With that I put any money I need for a week's worth of rent and a little for basic foods. Whatever I have left over is what I can spend that week. It means that some weeks I will have more and some weeks I will have less.**

ELUTIL: **I see. In fact, you could almost do that daily if you have to!**

BELESSUNU: **Kheruef said as much. But, he reminded me that some days I will go hungrier than other days and that starving oneself can make you extra hungry the next day. That's why it's good to know what you are likely to make weekly.**

ELUTIL: **BUT, knowledge is power. And the whole plan is based on your own effort and work. Amazing.**

BELESSUNU: **You are so smart! How are you doing on your budget?**

ELUTIL: **I know what I have for a week. Still, I have to remember to not keep all of the money with me every time I go out or I feel like I'm spending it too quickly. I finally decided to divide up the money I parsed for a week, into coins I can use for a day or two. That way, if I let some desire steal from me today, I will still have tomorrow to try to do better. And I won't have stolen from tomorrow's money.**

BELESSUNU: **I like that idea. With all of this knowledge, I think I will get back to where I was before my unfortunate lapse in judgment in record time. I also find that once I'd lost a lot of my money, I'm more likely to guard how I spend it now. It's almost as if I needed to learn that lesson the hard way.**

ELUTIL: **I, personally, hope to learn from your experience. I'm grateful you stopped in today because it gives me a clearer idea about saving.**

The two women chatted on about Elutil's business. By the end, Elutil had decided to rent a small table for Belessunu's jewelry. Elutil would collect the money from the jewelry that she sold and give a portion of the money to Belessunu. They both parted feeling like they had both won.

Generalization:

Values and Goals – these two concepts walk hand in hand when making a budget. And your decisions are no less complicated than it was for the characters in the story. If you value your freedom, you make goals that put that freedom front and center. If you value your time spent at home with your family, your goals will be quite different from the freedom seeker.

The similarities are in the need to save to achieve your goals. Like to travel? That will take money. Want a cabin in the mountains you can escape to? Money. Want a small boat for fishing on a local lake? Money. Want to pay off debt? Money. Want to take eco-trips and help restore a forest in a far-flung land? Money. Want to scuba dive off the coast of Australia at the Great Barrier Reef? Money. Want to add to your existing home and make your place a senior dog rescue? Money. Want to develop a homeless shelter in a vacant lot nearby? Money.

All of the above (and your goals, too) will need varying amounts of cash. So, figure out what is most important to you (your values) and how you'd like to put them into place (your goals).

Budgeting 101:

Kheruef's simple budget explanation works. (But perhaps not for everyone.)

First, figure out how much you earn – after taxes – in a month. The money is your "take-home" pay. If you have over-time pay, you probably shouldn't include it because, like the characters, that income will change with the days or weeks or months.

Second, determine your fixed expenses. Typically that's your **rent/mortgage**, **auto loan**, and **student loan** repayments and **utilities**. [Usually – food isn't included in this because purchasing food can be quite flexible. Taco Tuesday is, by far, one of the best examples of that flexibility, even if Taco Tuesday isn't your thing. Buy a taco on any other day, and you'll pay two or three times as much.] However, many economists are adding **taxes**, **insurance**, and your **10% savings** account to this "fixed expenses" list. Families will tell you the costs for **babysitting** and **lawn care** should be put into the fixed expenses. And commuters would add gas and/or transportation costs (bus, train).

What's left over is for "flexible expenses", sometimes called "discretionary expenses." Discretionary means you have some choice in the matter. This category includes: food, clothing, entertainment, luxury items, nonessential goods (eg. flowers) and services (eg. spa treatments), and vacations.

Right now the equation looks like this:

INCOME – FIXED EXPENSES = FLEXIBLE EXPENSES

The "Allowance" Budget

All things being equal, the idea that Kheruef puts forward about dividing the Flexible Expenses into **four equal parts** and apportioning them to yourself may work for some people who are not good with budgets. Some economists liken it to **giving yourself an allowance**. You could turn that into cash, put it into four envelopes and make sure you don't cheat by diving into another envelope before the week is up.

But given that most people use credit cards or debit cards, this could be easier said than done. STILL, if you find that you overspend EVERY WEEK, try putting yourself on an allowance and let the limits sink in to your psyche about what IS and IS NOT a good way to spend your hard earned cash.

A More Traditional Budget

This budget requires that you keep track of all of your expenses and mark them down. (If you don't like the word "budget," try calling it your "spending plan.") Review how you spend your money by looking at your online tracking – you credit card statements and your bank statements. Try to put your expenses into categories like: FOOD, CLOTHING, ENTERTAINMENT. Decide which of those expenses could use a little self-control added to the mix and apply percentages you want spent on your categories.

We'll call your Flexible Expenses 100% of what you're allowed to divide up. So, let's say you will allow yourself to spend 50% on FOOD: eating out, and eating in, coffee, treats, fast-food, snacks, etc. That leaves you another 50% to divide between clothing and entertainment. If you would rather go shopping more than go to a movie, put a higher percentage on CLOTHING. If you'd rather go to the show/play/sports arena instead of buying clothes, put a higher percentage on ENTERTAINMENT. So, your end percentages could be 50%, 30%, 20%. Multiply your Flexible Spending by .5 for 50%, .3 for 30% and .2 for 20% to discover how much money in any given month you're allowed to spend. And, there you go! A spending plan!

Let's say you have $532.00 in your Flexible Expenses Category.
50% = $532 x .5 = $266.00 30% = $532 x .3 = $159.60 20%= $532 x .2 = $106.40

Just remember that it's YOUR budget and you're welcome to change those percentages if you realize you EAT OUT way more than you thought you did! Or, if you realize your goal is more important than that extra pair of shoes, put the shoe money in your savings!!

Budgets are great if you can keep on top of them!

The characters:
Elutil and Belessunu are both in the business of creating something and selling their wares. Belessunu has to start over saving because of her carelessness, but Kheruef makes it clear that she can still budget her money by parsing out what she actually makes to last for the week. Elutil grasps the concept easily. It is actually a behavior that we often do ourselves – bargaining with ourselves to spend money in one place while saving in another. The important difference is that they will be doing in purposely – they will be paying attention to how they spend their money. And THAT is half the battle!

The Sixth Step
Invest in Your Home and Your Family

KHERUEF: **We are now to the 6th step. If you are setting aside one out of ten coins and can put away even more without it being a detriment to your wellbeing, then your coins will grow that much faster! From here on out, we will be talking about moving you into your future.**

KHERUEF: **Don't forget to invest in yourselves and your property and your family. Many of you have families and it would be wrong to spend all of your coins on trinkets or trips away while your family lives in unclean and poor surroundings. If you pay a landlord rent for your dwelling, consider buying your own home. Then invest in your home and surroundings so that it will be a good, peaceful place to raise your children.**

KHERUEF: **A good home offers a person gladness. To be able to eat the figs from your own tree, and to raise a few chickens for their eggs insures that the hard times will not be so hungry. Grapes dangling from the garden wall, herbs to enhance a meal … these all will brighten your mood and that of your family. And your spouse will be grateful that the children have a clean home and room to play and learn under your own roof.**

ENLIL: **How are we to get the money for this?**

KHERUEF: **The moneylenders are happy to loan money for this. It means that you are stable and likely to stay in the area. You can look around to see who will rent his money for a good price. The money lender will be more likely to loan you money if you can provide a good part of the coins yourself and may look upon you more kindly.**

KHERUEF: When your house is built, or bought, you can pay the moneylender much the same way as you paid your landlord, only that money will be going toward the investment you have made in yourself and your family. Eventually, you will have paid off the moneylender and so be free of that debt. The only cost will be Ptolemy's taxes.

ISHTAR: **Should we buy a grand home to show that we have wealth?**

KHERUEF: **Buy a home that is within your means. Never purchase what you think you will never be able to pay for. There is no shame in owning a smaller home if it is well cared for and a glad tiding to visitors. But a home that is overly large with no one to keep it clean or to take care of surrounding lands is a sure sign of someone living outside their means. Try not to be someone you are not.**

ISHTAR: **So, then, as we get richer, we can buy another, larger house?**

KHERUEF laughs: **I recommend it! And, if you are wise with your coins and good at management, you can rent the old house and become the landlord!**

MANY **nods and happy noise.**

KHERUEF: **Once free of the debt on your house, you will have more money to put aside to invest in other things. So, the 6th step is to own your own home.**
KHERUEF: **Your job is to wander about your neighborhood and see what a home like yours might cost to buy. And, then go to a different part and ask the same questions. I want you to figure out how much money you think you'd like to spend to get the house you want. And, more than that, to think about saving to buy a house someday.**

Outside, Marduk and Lugal paused and waited for Nammu to finish talking to Kheruef. When he came out, Marduk and Lugal walked purposely up to the home-builder.

MARDUK: **I was wondering if we could talk a bit.**

LUGAL: **Apparently, great minds think alike, for I wanted a bit of your time, too.**

NAMMU: **What's on your minds?**

They gestured to each other and finally Lugal spoke.

LUGAL: **I'm not sure where to start, but I thought you could go through a quick list of things to look for in a well-built house.**

MARDUK: **Exactly! I want to know that what I'm looking at is what I need to be looking at!**

NAMMU: **I tell you what. Come to my house and I'll show you the special things I did to make sure my house was good enough for me. If you want, we can go right now.**

MARDUK AND LUGAL: **Let's go!**

NAMMU: I live in a simple but elegant home on the east side. I'm not particularly fond of decoration as part of the building, but I do like airy doors and sturdy walls. I bought the property after I started to make money making furniture and then built the house the way I wanted, slowly but surely. My wife and children have plenty of room and the house is comfortable.

LUGAL: It sounds nice! Is there land around it?

NAMMU: Yes, but it's not visible at first. The house is wide, side to side, and it covers up a yard I have in the back. In this way, it looks like what other people around me have, but what the people don't see is what makes the property special.

The three walked through town talking about their wives and children. They each told how they'd come to live in the house they were currently in, and parts of their house that they liked and didn't like. Nammu mentioned a few solutions to problems and even commented on things that likely couldn't be fixed.

The closer they got to Nammu's house, the more date palms there were that lined the roads. This meant that if you walked in just the right place, you could have a little shade and relief from the sun, and then some sun in between. It was quite pleasant.

As they got closer to Nammu's house, they could catch glimpses of the Nile River. The area now seemed to be quite lush. Here and there were homes with front yards filled with pomegranate trees, olive trees and even an occasional cedar tree brought all the way from Assyria. Nammu's house was at the end of a street – beyond which were fields of wheat and barley as far as the eye could see in either direction. No doubt, the river was glistening just past the crops.

Rather than taking them to see the house first, he walked them around the far right end of the house to his back yard. A stone's throw from the house was a four foot high wall that marked his yard from the fields.

Marduk stopped and crossed his arms.
MARDUK: Why is the wall so high?

LUGAL laughed: I think I know, but please, tell us before I sound like a fool!

NAMMU: The wall is built into the ground another 4 feet. It is there to protect against the inundation of the Nile. Only once while I have been living here has the wall failed me. And, then I had to rebuild parts of my house. Other people are not so lucky since they don't have my skills!

MARDUK: Clever!

LUGAL: **I noticed that you have several gardens. There are melons meandering about, and on the shady side of the house, it looks like you grow herbs and lettuce in raised gardens. And, you've got plums and even a lemon from India!**

NAMMU: **My wife's mother lives with us and she tends to that garden. She is older now and has trouble bending over, so I made that raised garden so that she can still manage it. She adds many flavors to our diet. We owe her for our delicious meals! The lemon tree was her idea, too. As a child, she remembered having lemon squeezed onto cooked vegetables and my wife was able to find a tree for her.**

MARDUK: **You do, indeed, have a wide house!**

NAMMU: **It's easy to see here. I only wanted a one-story house. From the front it looks to be a little over three rooms wide. But you can see that I attached more rooms at the back. One is for the children and one is for my wife's mother. Our bedroom is next to the children's room and the other 2 rooms are family rooms - the kitchen and where we eat and gather.**

Nammu motioned for them to come closer. He showed them that most of the rooms were connected by large breezy doorways that made it possible to walk almost all the way from one end of the house to the other. The doorways had breeze-cloths which could be dampened. Some of the walls had built in benches, but most were filled with Nammu's homemade furniture.

A woman came through the doorway and smiled at her husband.

NAMMU: **This is my wife, Aria. Aria, these are new friends of mine from the class I'm taking in the city.**

ARIA: **I'm happy to meet my husband's friends. Can I bring you some tea? Please have a seat at the table outside and I'll bring you something.**

LUGAL: **That would be quite nice. I still have many questions for your husband and, no doubt, I will need something to wet my tongue before I'm done!**

ALL **Laugh.**

They went back outside to a table in the shade of two fig trees. Nammu walked over, pulled off a fig and popped it into his mouth. He motioned to the others to do the same.

They settled down at the table and Marduk and Lugal commented on the arrangement of the house and the yard.

Soon, Aria brought out cups of tea along with a tray filled with chopped dates, figs, plums, and grapes. She also brought out some homemade flat bread used to wrap around the fruits along with some honey to sweeten the treat. Aria demonstrated how to eat this curious dessert and the two men declared it a wonderful indulgence.

ARIA: **We have such wealth of fruit here at our home, I always need to come up with a new way to serve it. Enjoy!** ***(she leaves)***

Throughout the next hour, Marduk and Lugal asked about house construction, doorway construction and what to look for in lintels, what direction the doors should face to get a breeze through the house, the use of windows, built in benches, bricks vs. rock as building blocks, building double and triple walls to keep the house cool, the use of trees to shade the house and keep it cooler still, two floors vs. one floor, to build or not to build a courtyard, and using reed roofing for the outdoors.

At the end of the conversation, Marduk and Lugal were filled with ideas. They would each have to decide if they could ever have a house like Nammu's, but when they learned that he had built the house one building at a time, they both thought that it was do-able.

MARDUK: **This is something I might be able to do one day. I first need to buy some land. And, I just might call on you to build my first house! That would be grand. Then, I could save some more money and add on. I would never have to leave my home. I could just keep adding!**

LUGAL: **I agree. I don't have a big need to move away. I just want something comfortable to call my own. And, you've made a big house out of a small one! I like the ideas you've given us today. Thank you!**

NAMMU: **You are most welcome. Can I please ask a favor? Don't tell anyone where I actually live. You may tell of the experience, but I would rather not have a lot of people come looking just to see my little big house. YOU BOTH, however, are welcome to come see me again!**

MARDUK: **I understand. You have a little gem here. Someday, I want to create my own little gem!**

LUGAL: **I too understand. Marduk and I probably need to leave you now and do the rest of our homework. Please thank your wife for us.**

Nammu, Marduk and Lugal said their goodbyes and Marduk and Lugal talked about all they had seen as they made their way back into town.

Historical notes

Homes for middle and lower class were usually made of hand-made mud bricks dried in the sun. Sometimes the walls were two or three bricks thick – as if someone had made the first wall, and a second wall right next to it and a third wall next to that. This kept the heat out – as much as is possible! The usual house was a square divided into two or three rooms. Rarely, rock was used. Many homes had a second floor with an open "apartment" on the roof for sleeping. It was covered with a woven reed mat. Some homes may have been covered with an outer layer of mud to cover cracks. This may have been painted.

It was common for homes to have a garden for growing every day vegetables and herbs. Other oddities would have been brought to Egypt along the trade routes. A cedar tree from Assyria, a lemon from India, and peaches from Persia were not unheard of in Ancient Egypt.

As an aside … homes built in the United States in the 1940s and 1950s were often small. If a person had purchased one and later needed more room, they often made additions to the home – a bedroom over a garage, for instance. Then they'd add on more and more rooms until the house was able to serve the parents, the kids and all the activities that come with a family!

Generalization:

Start small and work your way up. Don't live like a rich person, overextend yourself and then have to pay dearly to get yourself out of trouble.

In the case of housing, sometimes renting is PERFECT for what you need. But, if you find yourself wanting to live in a place where you're allowed to make changes - a particular color on the walls that a landlord won't want, or an addition you'd like to make to a building, or you're starting a family with no place to grow – then, you might want to think about buying a house. Most of the time, you'll need a down payment – perhaps substantial! If you've been squirreling money away, then this could be the time to use it. But you can probably cross buying a house off your list if you have no savings.

So, buying a house is really contingent on you coming to grips with the prior lessons here. Saving money, curbing your spending, protecting yourself from predators … they're all part of the greater picture.

Right Now

Today, you could start training yourself to grow some of your own food. What with all of the advances in hydroponics, you could do it without soil and with very little space. Or, you could try growing herbs you like to use – say, cilantro – in a pot on the porch. If you're really bad at growing things, NOW is the time to figure out what plants you can get along with. Some are outrageously easy to grow and others take time, love and attention. I won't tell anyone about your failures with plants! Trust me – I've had many. But there are a few I adore and grow every summer – porch tomatoes being one. So teach yourself how to do it while you don't have a model house to show off. That way, when you get your first home, you'll already know how to make the front door, or the back porch, inviting!!

As for trees, there are the mini-me versions that are fine for growing in large pots. They're called "dwarf trees" and they can still give you great tasting fresh fruit. You will need a bit of space for the top of the tree to grow, but they won't really outgrow your pot until you plant them in the ground. And, dwarf versions never really get as big as the original tree anyway. I'm telling you – there's a dwarf tree out there with your name on it!!

The characters:

Marduk and Lugal seek the advice of someone they know who builds homes for a living. You should do the same. If you have cultivated friends who have bought homes, or who arrange loans, or who actually build homes, learn all you can from them. Ask questions, but don't forget to "pay" for their kindness by doing the things that maintain your normal friendship or relationship to them. Later, if you aren't using your friends for their skills, you will have the knowledge they gave you to start your own home buying adventure.

The Seventh Step
Prepare for the Future

KHERUEF: **Good day! Your job last week was to look into the prices of homes in your area and elsewhere. Did anyone have any great insight into this process?**

ENLIL: **I noticed that homes with more surrounding land cost more and that homes that seemed to be the same on the outside cost about the same amount of coins. I considered that a good sign in judging what I might like to buy someday in an area.**

KHERUEF: **I can see you were thinking of a place to grow crops, perhaps wheat? Good. And, Enlil, were you aware that you can also purchase land? Without buying a house?**

ENLIL: **I knew, but as I looked I found out more and more about that process, too. This class has opened up a whole new way of looking at things! Thank-you!**

MANY: **Here! Here! Well said! True! Thank you!**

KHERUEF: **Good tidings to you all! If I have made you think about managing your money and valuing your worth, then it has done what Pharaoh Ptolemy wanted. But we're not done yet!**
KHERUEF: **This is the final step. You all have had many things to think about. And, while many of you are yet young, you may not have thought about the obvious.**

KHERUEF: **Everyone's life starts when they are young and proceeds to old age. No one escapes this path unless the gods call him or her early. So, it is important to make preparations for the days to come. You will need a suitable income when you are no longer able to work. You will also want to make preparations for your family when you are no longer capable of providing for them. This lesson will instruct you for the coming days.**

KHERUEF: **The person, because of his understanding of the laws of wealth, will know about investing and should acquire throughout the ages of man, a surplus. He should plan for certain investments that will keep on working for many years past his life.**

LUGAL: **Can I get a sturdy chest and bury my money?**

KHERUEF: **That <u>may</u> not be a bad idea, but once you visit this chest, it will be known and will become the loot of thieves. And, a chest buried may be forgotten or unknown if you were taken before your time and then the money would go unused.**

LUGAL: **So, you don't recommend it?**

KHERUEF smiles kindly: **Not really. Maybe in the beginning, but later on, No.**

KHERUEF: **However, you could purchase land or houses as a way to "keep" this money useful. If the land and houses are chosen carefully they may increase in value and serve the same purpose as burying the coins. Then, in the future, one of your children could sell the house or property thereby gaining its worth.**

MARDUK: **That would be burying the money in an investment and hiding it in plain sight!**

ALL laugh.

KHERUEF: **Good! And, don't forget that you can rent the houses and property you own, so that as you grow older you will still be making money from them. As I mentioned before, you can become the landlords!!**

KHERUEF: **Another choice you might make is to rent your money to a moneylender. And as time goes by, increase the amount so as to get more in rent!**

NAMMU: **I have a friend who is a silversmith. He does that exactly! He never seems to run out of money and can now pay for his own silver from the deposit of coins he made so long ago. I always wondered how that worked. But I can see that he is simply making his money work for him – the way you mentioned at the beginning.**

KHERUEF: **Indeed. Not many think to lend the moneylender money … but who knows better about renting money than he? It's true! Given the return for so little effort at the start, it is an easy way to save for when you are old and everyone should do it. Better that than to be old and in a pitiful state or a burden to your family.**

KHERUEF: **You've learned how to save one of ten coins and to budget and control your expenses. And while it's good to have more coins, it won't make you rich. You must now consider putting your money to work for you! Now you begin to earn your fortunes and I will teach you one last lesson.**

MARDUK: **So, we worked for our coins and now they must work for us! Tell us more!**

ALL nod and lean in to hear.

KHERUEF explains: **Now you will learn how to invest your money in another business. It's not as easy as it sounds. In my first investment, I lost everything! I had**

to start with the 1st and 2nd steps and save and budget all over. But I learned from my mistake and it wasn't long before I started investing again.

PUZU: **You've had to start from the beginning … twice? But even now you're the richest man in Egypt? That's amazing.**

KHERUEF: **It's important to understand that I wasn't exactly starting over because I already had the good habits of saving and budgeting. I didn't have to struggle with my desires the way I had in the beginning – much as some of you are since you're still at the start.**

PUZU and the rest nodded.

KHERUEF: **Let me tell you of my first profitable investment. I made a loan to a shield maker. Once a year, he would purchase large amounts of bronze for making his shields. And he would make that bronze last throughout the year. Since he didn't have enough money to buy it all in the beginning, I loaned him enough money to pay the merchants. He was an honorable man and I knew he would repay me. When he had sold enough, he would pay me back the original amount. He would also pay me rent on the money I loaned him, so every time he sold a shield, he would give me a small rental payment. That meant that I always had a trickle of coins coming back to me. Therefore, not only did my money return to me, but my earnings increased, too!**

MARDUK: **How did you have enough money to give him in the first place? That bronze must have cost a lot!**

KHERUEF smiled at the man: **I had saved enough that I could give him that much. It was all from being willing to forego extra helpings of bread, I believe. It took me a while, but I could see the usefulness of saving that many coins, the first time I invested well!**

NAMMU: **How long was it before you got any of your money back?**

KHERUEF: **It was about 2 months – from the time he spent the money and returned with the bronze to the time he sold his first shield - for his first money-rent payment. Then, it was another couple of months until I got the investment money back. Even still, I received rent until the next time I loaned him a large amount the following year.**

KHERUEF looked at the entire group, saying: **The coins in your possession will increase rapidly once you make good choices for investment. Your assignment today and in the coming weeks and months, is to see who you might invest in and what business they have. Put your coins to work so that you may have gold aplenty.**

KHERUEF CLOSES THE LESSONS: **So, here's the plan for your future.**

Save one in ten coins. If there comes a time when you can save more, then the faster your wealth will grow.

Control your expenses by weeding out frivolous desires and budget your coins carefully.

Compare the prices of items and spend wisely.

Invest in yourself by learning to be the best at your trade. Invest in your family that all may stay strong and healthy and live a good life.

Buy your own home, and after doing that, purchase other homes and property that may increase with value over time. Rent them to people so that your income will be increased.

Give money to a moneylender and gather the earnings on the rent so that when you are old and gray you will have an income and will not be a burden on others or alone and pitiful.

And, finally, invest in worthy enterprises. Start small. Then as you get more coins, invest again, and more. Protect your investing by learning more about the person and the business.

And, lest anyone here forget, be sure to guard your wealth and keep it safe.

EVERYONE**: (The class gave a loud hearty round of applause.)**

Kheruef paused as he watched people mingle. And, upon realizing that he had invested so much of his time and energy in this class, he knew that he'd enjoyed this as much as they had.

KHERUEF: **But wait! Before you leave I must tell you how I lost the money the first time so you will not make the same mistake.**
They ALL sat back down.

KHERUEF: **I believed that if I invested in a trader, that I might get my money back in large amounts. One trader I knew, who was just starting, decided to make a trip to the edge of Bactria high in the mountains. There he would purchase large stones with a blue in them as blue as the sea. Perhaps you have heard of Lapis Lazuli?**

Some people nodded their heads.

KHERUEF: **It is used in Egypt to adorn the death masks of its mightiest pharaohs. It is worth a king's ransom! I gave the trader my money and he said he would split the profits earned from the take. It sounds good, right? Many months passed and after a year, I knew my money was gone. When he at last came back to Egypt, he was bent and old and wounded. He had been captured by the tribes, made to work as a slave and all his money and goods taken in part because he was not well known and he had tried to make trades that the tribes were not happy with. When he returned, he barely even remembered me and sought shelter with an aging sister. He died shortly afterward. With no way to get my money back, I knew it was gone forever. I realized the error in my decision.**

KHERUEF continued: **Choose the person and the business wisely. Try not to think of ONE investment as the SINGLE investment you will make. And, if you suffer the same fate as me, you all KNOW HOW TO START OVER just as I did. You must rely on yourselves more than others. So, do not blame others for YOUR misjudgment about a person's worth or blame anyone for a calamity that happens to them. The gods give and the gods taketh away. You must learn to live with some unpredictability in finances even as our beloved Nile River teaches us.**

KHERUEF: (solemnly raises his hand) **Go forth and prosper.**

ALL: **Go forth and prosper!!**

Generalization:
Kheruef didn't know about "flipping homes" or he might have suggested that as a way to make money! Still, let's take a closer look at his archaic language and see if we can understand what he wants his students to invest in.

Buying property
His first line of investment is rather old school. First you buy a house (or a condo), you outgrow it, and use it as your first rental even as you're buying a new house. Plenty of people do that. If you're handy with tools and you're good at management, you could expect to get a good sum of money on your property. If you would have to hire someone to fix something every time something went wrong, well.... then.... after a while it might not be so profitable. There are plenty of management companies who can do all of that for you – for a price. Kheruef suggests that rental income is a way to supplement your retirement. Since "everyone's life proceeds to old age", he asks his students to consider how they want to take care of the costs that come with that.

He also refers to the heirs being able to sell the house. That's another way to see a profit down the line if you invest in property and housing. And, perhaps at the point when you're ready to sell the house, the income from it will be helpful to your retirement.

Loaning money to the moneylenders

His second line of investment is to loan your money to the moneylenders. Nowadays, the basic way to do that is put your money in a savings account. Your money doesn't just sit there. The banks invest it in low-risk investments and one way the banks return the favor is to give you some of that earned investment income back to you. Usually savings accounts don't have very high yields. In other words, they won't make you much money.

There are other options that you will need to look into. Certificates of Deposit (CDs) are a federally insured savings account with a fixed interest rate and a fixed date of withdrawal. If you don't need that money right away and can wait 5 to 10 years before accessing those funds, this is a relatively safe way to "lend money to the moneylenders". IF you HAVE to withdraw, there's a hefty penalty. If you can wait, the interest rate is higher than a regular savings account.

One more type of lending money to the moneylenders is called a Treasury Security. There are Treasury Bills, Treasury Bonds and even Savings Bonds. In the case of U.S. Treasury Securities, you are loaning money to the U.S. Federal Government. Like the CDs, they have a fixed interest rate and a fixed date of withdrawal. Bonds can be sold for a one year duration up to a 30 year duration. You'll have to talk to your broker about the cost of said item because it varies by your credit score.

Investing money in another business

We think of this as investing in the stock market. If you own stock in Home Depot, you are essentially investing in that company and hoping that you will get your investment PLUS interest back when you sell the stock. This will usually require that you go through an Investment Firm which opens your investment account. You give them money and pay their fees and they invest in stocks that you ask for, or ones they think you should have based on your risk tolerance.

You could always invest in a friend's startup company as Kheruef explained it. Sometimes the magic works and sometimes it doesn't. Just remember, nothing is guaranteed however much your friend says it's a "sure thing." Kheruef failed on his first venture, but succeeded on his second. And he reminded his students, "If you fail, you will already know how to start over.

Ancient Glossary

Burden of desire – the weight in your heart (burden) of wanting something terribly badly, plus the cost of "feeding" (giving into) that want (desire)

Casual Desires vs Cherished Desires – A Casual Desire is one that comes and goes and is more "relaxed." In the case of the story, it would refer to something a person might like but wouldn't feel like he/she/they HAD TO HAVE. A Cherished Desire is something you've hoped for for a long time. In the story, it would refer to the character Qishti who wants to live like the people he serves.

Coins – money

Craftsmanship – the quality and skill in a particular craft, eg. Building homes, making jewelry

Drinking or eating your savings – refers to a habit of drinking or eating that can't be broken. Verges on addictive behavior.

Feeding your desires – giving into your wants

Hapi - an Egyptian god of fertility who brought the rich silt with the Nile's flood to enrich the land. He was represented by water, the lotus and the growing papyrus plant. Hence, if you were a business person, you might worship Hapi to have him bring you wealth that flowed like water to you.

Having your desires steal your money (things that steal your money) – If you don't really have a whole heck of a lot of money and you buy things you want, then that thing, in effect, steals money you don't really have from you!

Lintels – a horizontal support across the top of a door that spans from one side of the door to the next. Before the advent of steel and in Ancient Egypt before wood was easily available, the lintel was often the weakest point in a mudbrick home.

Loaning coins to the moneylender – When coins (money) were loaned to the moneylender (banker), the moneylender paid rent (interest) on the money

Masquerading – pretending to be someone you're not by wearing clothes and accessories and adopting the style or pretense of that person

Moneylender – a banker

One in ten – 10%

Purse - Heavy vs Lean – a purse is simply a place to put money. A heavy purse is one with plenty of (heavy) coins in it. In other words, full. A lean (skinny) purse is one with hardly any coins in it.

Practice discretion – behaving and talking in such a way that you don't reveal private information

Renting money – borrowing money as part of a loan that includes, essentially, interest on the loan. In other words, you pay MORE than what you borrow to have the privilege of having that money NOW.

Storehouse – a place (often large) where items are stored (saved). This is similar to a warehouse where goods (wares) are housed or kept.

Surplus – more than enough of something

Trades and jobs – a trade is a job where a certain skill set is needed and this often requires advanced training. A job is a position of regular employment. So, in the case of the Pottery stall in the story, the person working in the booth has a job. The Potter, her sister, has a trade.

Values and goals – a value is what a person considers to be important in his/her/their life. A goal is the object of a person's ambition, effort, or aim. The goal is determined by one's values.

Contemporary Glossary

Budget – a probable income and expenses plan aimed at helping a person make informed decisions about cash flow

Clothing – clothes, but also the things one puts on oneself such as clothes, accessories, etc as far as a budget is concerned

Comparison shopping – the practice of comparing prices for items, as well as services, from different vendors and retail stores before buying

Discretionary spending – money spent on non-essential items such as vacations, or luxury items

Disposable income – the income left after taxes and other fixed expenses

Dwarf trees - a tree grafted to a dwarfing root stock that remains smaller than the original tree and has a more compact growth habit. This makes fruit easier to reach and the trees easier to trim and care for.

Entertainment – something done for amusement or enjoyment

Economy – the wealth and resources of a country especially related to the production and purchase of goods

Evaporative cooling – the resulting cooling because of the evaporation of a liquid – usually water

Expenditures – the amount of money spent or the result of spending money

Experiences vs repetition – a novel encounter vs a thing repeated

Finances – in personal terms, the amount of money you manage

Fixed expenses – a cost of something that doesn't go up or down (fixed) given there are no changes in the mix. In terms of personal finances, items like rent at the same place, the cost of insurance, leases, payments and loans usually stay the same, until they don't. (Say, a rent increase.)

Flexible expenses – the costs of items that can be changed, reduced or eliminated altogether.

Food – any nutritious substance that a human (or animal) will or can eat. Theoretically, the best kind of food provides fiber, vitamins, minerals, protein, energy or a combination of these for a healthful life and growth.

Hydroponic gardens – the process of growing plants in water (or other non-soil) by adding nutrients and light

Income – money received for work or investments

Invest in yourself/family – devoting time, effort and energy to making a better life for yourself and your family

Investments – the action of putting money toward some process for a return – a profit or some kind of material

Needs – things that are necessary; of necessity

Pay stub – a piece of paper given with every employee's paycheck with the earned amount and information about what was deducted – taxes, social security (FICA or SS), and insurance

Price of convenience – the cost of being able to purchase/get something with little to no effort. For instance, dinner bought at a fast food restaurant, coffee bought at a drive-through, groceries delivered to your door, etc. But the word "price" also indicates the loss of human interaction, the loss of mutual understanding, the increased sense of aloneness, etc that comes with the ease and lack of effort.

Self-discipline – the ability to control one's feelings and sense of weakness and to go after what one knows to be right, despite the temptations.

Take-home pay – the actual amount of the paycheck that gets deposited into your bank account or is given to you in cash.

Taxes and fees – money you must contribute to the city, county, state, or nation to keep said municipalities solvent

Training – the action you take to increase your skills, abilities, or types of behavior (especially in sports or athletics)

Upscale and downscale – upscale = expensive and designed to appeal to rich consumers; downscale, in the context of "upscale" = inexpensive and designed to fill a need in less affluent neighborhoods or to appeal to poorer communities

Values and goals – values – a person's principals or standards of behavior. Goals – the object of a person's ambition or effort – generally driven by one's values

Wants – those items which a person desires to possess – from simple… a candy bar - - to complex … a 1982 DeLorean DMC-12.

What the market will bear – prices set that the vast majority of consumers in an area will be able to pay. Given that, some areas are prime for overpricing because of location, location, location.

Win-win situations – the result of something is good for everyone involved. This may involve a compromise, but the outcome is acceptable.

APPENDIX

Worksheets

Save One in Ten – Percentages in Money Name ____________________________

Following the pattern from the story of figuring out 10% of an amount of money, move the decimal point one to the left and leave only two numerals to the right of the decimal point.

Verbal Example: $43.72 – move the decimal to the left and you've got $4.372. Remove the last numeral so you only have two numerals after the decimal point, and you now have your answer: 10 % = $4.37.

Visual Example: **$43.72** **$43.72** **$4 3.72** **$4.372** **$4 . 37~~2~~**
ANSWER: 10% = **$4.37**

Find ten percent of each of these numbers.

$873.45 = __________ $1033.09 = __________ $55.00 = __________

$1094.66 = ________________ $1300.98 = _______________

$3361.42 = _________________ $9055.23 = _________________

Price tags without decimals

Let's say you go to a swap meet, flea market, tag sale, garage sale, yard sale (insert name of outdoor market in your state!) and people only have tags on an item that have no decimal points. Or, maybe YOU are the one selling an item and YOU put tags/stickers on something with no decimal points. Either way, for some reason, you need to find 10% of an item – perhaps to put away for your savings! The question is – WHERE DOES THAT DECIMAL GO??

$5 $15 $20 These become $5.00, $15.00, $20.00

If these tags were written in standard notation, you would put the decimal at the END of the number shown and add two zeros.

To find 10%, you would use the same process as you did at the top of this worksheet. Try it here. First write the standard notation and then the percent. Be sure to only have two numbers after the decimal when you're all done.

$8 = ___________ 10% = ______________

$12 = ____________ 10% = ____________

$23 = ____________ 10% = ______________

$85 = ____________ 10% = ____________

Let's take a look at prices that really mean something else. Anytime a vendor puts $3.99 on an item, they really mean $4.00. It's a way of beating the prices other vendors have. If you buy LOTS of a product, the savings could be useful. Otherwise, a penny isn't much to save these days.

Rounding up to solve the 10% issue.

Verbal example - $4.99 rounds up to $5.00. Moving the decimal to the left one place gives you .500. Remove the final zero and you have $.50 or 50 cents. If you'd done 10% of $4.99, you'd find that the answer is 49 cents. I suggest you just put two quarters, or 50 cents, somewhere safe instead of one quarter, two dimes and four pennies in your jar.

Visual example -$4.99 ≈ $5.00   10% = .10 x 5.00 = .500   .50~~0~~ = 50cents

This method works well for other numbers over the 50 cent mark like $6.87 or $10.65, so go ahead and round up numbers that are over 50 cents (.50) and save that 10%!!

Try these:

Round up To nearest dollar	New Number	10% or times .10
$24.99	_________	____________
$3.75	_________	____________
$87.77	_________	____________

Needs and Wants – Are you trapped? Name ________________________

In the story, Belessunu notices that people see what others are wearing and want the same (or similar) thing. Have you seen this in yourself? A friend comes by wearing a new trendy cap, t-shirt, pair of shorts, shirt, dress, pair of shoes … whatever. Do you find yourself wanting the same thing (or a similar thing?) Briefly describe a time when this happened to you.

____

____

In the story, Enlil tells about people who will look over the bread and try to find a larger piece than someone who just bought a piece. Have you seen yourself in this? Your cousin, sister, brother, aunt, uncle, Dad, Mom … whoever … comes by with a large piece of pizza, cookie, piece of pie, scoop of ice cream, bag of chips (or similar thing) and you find yourself hopping up to see if you can get the same thing only bigger? Briefly describe a time when this happened to you.

____

____

In the story, Ishtar sells hand-crafted knives. Let's just see it as a specialty item for the purposes of these questions. Has someone ever told you that they have the newest game, the latest phone, the next generation bike/skateboard/scooter/motorcycle/skates/whatever? And, have you then hoped to get it – if not just outright gone and gotten it? Briefly describe a time when this happened to you.

____

____

Wants and desires are described as a beast that steals your earnings. What is the benefit of calling these behaviors a beast?

____

And, why might it be bad to call those behaviors a "beast"? What could be a problem with that?

____

Do you think you could call the wants and desires a "beast" and actually make progress in stopping the behaviors? Or, are you the sort of person who might "feed the beast"?

___

___

Decide if you are the sort to "tame the beast" or "feed the beast" and make a decision here about what you will do with this knowledge about yourself.

___

___

___

After you finish writing your answers, discuss what you think it means to WANT TO HAVE something someone else has so badly that you will find yourself thinking about it a lot, or whining/being moody about not having what that person has, or not talking to that person for a while, or talking to that person WAY TOO MUCH, or being rude to people because they HAVE what you don't/can't have. Are you trapped? Are your WANTS stealing money from you? Are they stealing your integrity? Put a few notes here before you start discussing.

___

___

___

___

Needs and Wants – New Experiences Name ______________________

Psychologists and Sociologists all tell us that having money and spending money aren't the keys to happiness. Sure, sure, it may be fun to go shopping or to a ball game, but when people are asked after they're grown up, or they are near the ends of their lives, what they remember most, they don't recall the times they went shopping or the time they got a new game, or all the baseball games they went to (unless it was THAT once in a lifetime one) or whatever. They recall experiences they had with their friends and family.

When we repeat certain experiences, like going to a pub week after week, or visiting the mall once a week with friends, or eating out at your favorite restaurant over and over, the repetition "steals" the newness from us. Like an old piece of clothing that we've worn to threads, or a tattered toy we have loved too much, or a book we've read over and over so that the pages are falling out, we miss out on new experiences that we'll tell about when we get older. Yes, those old things are comforting and comfortable. And I would never advocate that you get rid of that piece of clothing, toy or book. Perhaps, however, I would suggest that you "change it up" with unfamiliar, involving, connecting pursuits. Develop an "I'll try that!" attitude.

Research your city and the surrounding areas for some of the following:
Museums
____

Race tracks (to watch and small cars to race in)
____

Vietnamese/French/Persian (or something you've never had) restaurants
____

Libraries______________________________________

Parks____

Hiking _______________________________________
Trails____

Snorkeling/swimming/archery lessons (whatever)
____

Painting/cooking classes

Martial Arts classes

Yoga studios

Spas

Small Theme parks / water parks

Indoor/outdoor rock climbing

Plays to go to – local theaters

Add your own

Think of people who you'd like to take with you and invite them to try something new with you!

Imagine what the experience COULD be like!

Needs and Wants – No or Low-Cost Fun Name ________________________

Qishti says, "Everything costs money!" And, indeed, sometimes it feels like it. But when you were growing up, your parents did fun things with you that cost little to nothing. Otherwise, they could not have survived.

I'm only partly suggesting that you go back to doing some of those child-like things part of the time. Plenty of adults still fly kites, hike, play volley ball/frisbee at the park, walk the dog while seeking out new and interesting places, go to the beach/lake to swim or fish, and go on picnics.

Spend some time reminiscing about fun times you've had.

Write about memorable times that didn't cost all that much money. Sure – going to the Grand Canyon was fun, but it required time and cash. (Though there are ways to go that make it cheaper.) Then circle the events and try to remember just what made that event special.

____

____

____

____

____

____

____

____

____

What makes an event special for me?

____

____

____

In the story, Puzu shows Nadin how to drink beer slowly and Nadin admits that he might like it. As a teen, I loved skiing – the faster the better. But after a bum knee tried to sideline me, I found that I could still really enjoy skiing much more slowly. I took more notice of my surroundings – the mountains, the trees, and so on. Write down a few experiences you like that you always do quickly and imagine what it might be like if you took it slowly.

Be sure to create moments for yourself that include those special things. And try to make sure they are low or no-cost to you.

Compare Before You Buy Name ___________________________

Store Shopping

Think of an common name brand item you buy - Barbie or Lego, Louis Vuitton bags, Nike shoes or clothes, For All Mankind or American Eagle Outfitters, Nintendo or Rockstar, S&W Canned Tomatoes or San Marzano, Perrier or La Croix. The list goes on. Make yourself a note (on your phone?) and the next time you visit a mall/grocery store/clothing store check the price on the items you've chosen.

Then, yes, it's true, GO OUT OF YOUR WAY to go to a different store. Perhaps even one in a neighborhood UNLIKE YOURS. Upscale/downscale – your choice. Record the prices. I think you will be surprised – and perhaps left scratching your head.

Is it MORE expensive in a "downscale" store than at your own store? (Or, less?) Or, is it *as you might suspect*, MORE expensive at an "upscale" store? What do you think accounts for the difference? Choose one of your items to write about.

____

____

____

____

Head scratching moments.

There are some items that are sold for LESS at a really rich neighborhood and some items that are sold for MORE in a poorer neighborhood. Did you find any? Why do you think manufacturers or store owners are willing to "take a hit" or "make a profit" by doing that?

____

____

____

Online Shopping

Do the same activity as **Store Shopping**, only look for items online. Don't forget, stores like Walmart and Target have an online presence these days, as do some grocery stores. (Be sure to include Luxury Department Stores like Bergdorf Goodman, Nordstrom, and Neiman Marcus.)

Try to figure out what the product costs and how much it would take to have it shipped to you. Do this for four products you were able to find at four different stores.

Item ____

Cost Item Store Shipping

____

____

____

____

Now look to see if any of the places (Walmart??) will let you pick it up **In Store** at no shipping cost (vs Amazon?)? What have you saved?

____

____

Price an item that you use regularly out over a month and over a year. How much could you save?

____

Invest in Yourself Name ________________________________

In order to invest in yourself, you must decide where you want to go in life. If you'd really like to be a hair stylist, it would be silly to study soil science. If you have one job, but would like to get a different job, then **seeking** out training for your first job may just "doom" you to have to stay there. (This is different from going to training your BOSS sends you to!)

Make a brief list of some of the jobs or careers you've ever thought you might like.

____

____

____

____

____

____

Think about your current job and look to see if any of the jobs above might dove-tail, or be an easy shift, with your current job. List some steps you can take to get where you want to go.

____

____

____

If the jobs above aren't even close to what you currently do, consider what kind of training you need.

____

____

____

If the job you currently have is "okay" to "perfect", and you know you can't leave right away, think about how you can go about making yourself the BEST at what you do. Don't assume you are the BEST! Try to think of things that can make you stand out in the crowd.

____

____

Remember, the people who you work for now could be writing your future letters of recommendation. You will want to make a good impression on them, even if they're hard to work with, even if this isn't your "forever" job, even if this job isn't a perfect fit. Your boss will be writing about your performance – not your "fit." If they write about your "fit" and it was a bad "fit," then the letter of recommendation may not be what you hope for!

Think about "Performance" vs "Fit." What kind of a person are you? Do you do your utmost to perform well? Or, are you a want to "fit in" sort of person. Knowing which way you lean might help you change your behavior!

Create a Budget – Values and Goals Name ______________________________

Values can be lofty ideals like freedom, courage, love, beauty, friendship, knowledge, wisdom, and pleasure. There are many more – search 'abstract nouns.'

Other values can be more down to earth and relative like security for your family, freedom from oppression, dignity in death, excellence in business. The attachment of a prepositional phrase – **for** your family, **from** oppression, **in** death, etc - adds your personal relationship to the value and is often easier to picture. Again, if you look up "prepositions" you'll find lists and more lists!

Think of the things you value. Look up those lists and string together the words that mean the most to you.

____ ____

____ ____

____ ____

Look at your values and see if you can establish a goal that secures/cements that value for you. If you said, "security for my family" then your goal might be to save enough money in case of emergencies. Put down your value again and with it write down a goal worthy of YOU. And don't forget – **the ultimate aim is to make a budget and save money towards a goal.** While a goal might be to "make more friends" that isn't something that having more money should solve. In fact, if your friends just love you because of your money, when the money dries up, so do most of those friends.

Value____

Goal ____

Value____

Goal____

____

This isn't the end. It's just a beginning. Revisit **this** page many times to see if what you wrote was just garbage or it truly still resonates with you. Remember – your goals can change.

Create a Budget – Doing the Math Name ____________________________

A Month's Worth of Money – Remember to NOT include overtime.

-If you get paid once a month, HALLELUJAH! You're done.

-If you get paid every two weeks, find two consecutive pay stubs or check on your online bank account for how much is deposited twice in a month.

-If you get paid every week, you'll need four consecutive pay stubs, or to check your online bank account for the four deposits in a month.

-If you get paid daily … and maybe you get paid "under the table" (the government doesn't know about this) … then you're going to have to get creative and start writing down a list of each day's pay. It will take a while, but if you truly need to budget, then it could be worth it!

<u>Use only the lines you need</u>. If you have to keep track daily, figure it out where you can keep it quiet and pretend it's only one pay stub. If you have more than one job, use the extra lines or create a few!

1st pay stub ______________ +

2nd pay stub ______________ +

3rd pay stub ______________ +

4th pay stub ______________ =

TOTAL __________________

> To make things flow more easily, the plus sign is on the right side (not the traditional left). So, you'd read it like:
> 1st pay stub, plus
> the 2nd pay stub, plus
> the 3rd pay stub plus
> the 4th pay stub equals
> The TOTAL

Even if you get paid irregularly – two times the first week, then none the second, then five times the third week and four times the last week – you'll need to figure out an approximate monthly pay amount. In the story, Belessunu essentially had to do this in chunks and figure out a budget based on two weeks. If you're living really close to your limit, you can make a budget based on one week, but the longer the term, the easier it is to stick to a budget.

FIXED EXPENSES

Fixed Expenses per month - Utilities worksheet – you may not have all of these

Rent/lease/mortgage ______________ +	phone ________________________ +
Auto Loan _______________________ +	gas (home) ___________________ +
Other Loans _____________________ +	water ________________________ +
Utilities ________________________ +	electricity ___________________ +
10% savings _____________________ +	garbage/waste _________________ +
Insurance _______________________ +	sewer/septic _________________ =
Other ___________________________ =	total _________________________

The Fixed Total ______________________________

If ever there was a time to realize why you might need a budget – LOOK AT THAT FIXED TOTAL!! Yikes!

Subtract the Fixed Total from the Pay Total to find your Flexible Total.

Pay Total ______________________ - Fixed Total __________________________ =

_________________________ This is your Flexible spending amount

CAUTION – If your Fixed Total is larger than your Pay Total, then you are "living above, or beyond, your means." You will need to earn more money or change the way you're living.

You did all of the above to find this Flexible amount. The larger this is, the more flexibility you have. The smaller it is, the more you will need to rein in your Wants and Desires. If you already have a small amount, controlling those Wants and Desires will be key to getting to your financial freedom.

Create a Budget – The Flexible Spending Pt 1   Name ___________________________

Figuring out what you REALLY value in the three main categories (FOOD, CLOTHING, ENTERTAINMENT) will show up now when you review your flexible expenses. Look at your credit card statements and your bank statements for clues as to what you actually spend your money on.

Regardless of how much you spend in any category, be sure to include the small items as well as the big items. FOOD - For instance, that coffee you buy every day adds up – even if you only spend $7.00 on each. That time you ran into a convenience store for a $2.00 Slurpee – add that one, too. Did you feel generous and buy a round of beers for everyone at your table? Add it in. Did you take $20 out of the teller so you could go to a Food Truck? Add that, too. AND – groceries from this store and that store. Add them up, too!

CLOTHING – Shoes? Add it in. Cheap flip flops at a local store? Add that. Shoe laces? Go ahead and add it. Dresses, pants, suits, shorts, summer hat, t-shirts, swimming suit/trunks, etc? Add them all!

ENTERTAINMENT – Buying the extras in a video game? Oooo – for sure put that on the list. Movies, plays, theater? Add it. Spa treatments? If you like it and it's not food or clothing PUT IT ON THIS LIST. Wait! Add that new hairstyle, hair color, weave!! Don't fool yourself – you ARE entertained by trying on a new look or showing off your new style! Video Game cartridge? DVD? Old school Vinyl? New TV, console, entertainment furniture? Add them all. Seriously, if it's not FOOD or CLOTHING – the buck stops here.

Other – Okay- that vitamin purchase probably ought to have gone into food. The medication? Ummm… if you have to buy it monthly, put it in the Other Category on Fixed Expenses. The car repair? Ugh … you probably have to have a car and that should have come from your emergency funds or maybe even your 10% Savings Account. Transfer that money. Crap Happens.

Use the worksheet columns below to help you figure out where you're spending your money.

FOOD List	CLOTHING List	ENTERTAINMENT List
______________	______________	______________
______________	______________	______________
______________	______________	______________
______________	______________	______________
______________	______________	______________
______________	______________	______________
______________	______________	______________
______________	______________	______________
______________	______________	______________
______________	______________	______________
______________	______________	______________
______________	______________	______________
Total $ ______________	Total $ ______________	Total $ ______________

Take a look at your lists. Do you recognize yourself? Does it match with what you already believe about yourself?

Tell yourself what you know or have discovered about yourself.

____

____

____

Create a Budget – The Flexible Spending Pt 2 Name ___________________________

Look at the three columns on the 1st Flexible Spending page. Which one is the biggest and which the smallest? I can almost guarantee for most people, FOOD is the biggest. To figure out the "basic" percentage of each of these, add them all together and divide each by the total. WAIT! I'm going to show you what I mean!!

To make an equation out of this, we're going to use ONLY THE FIRST LETTER of each. F = FOOD, C = CLOTHING and E = ENTERTAINMENT. Here's what add them all together looks like.

F + C + E = total flexible spending before budget

F + C + E = tfsbb

That's not too bad because you know what each of those letters stand for. Let's say that you spent $222 on FOOD. And the Total (tfsbb) was $367. Take the $222 and divide it by $367.

F ÷ tfsbb = percent $222 ÷ $367 = .604904632 and the number goes on and on

(Do this on your calculator and you MAY end up with a really long number. Don't panic.)

Do you remember the Generalization pages after the very FIRST lesson in the script? The ones where you had to multiply your pay by 10% or .10 in order to save one in ten? And, remember where you had to get rid of everything but the two numerals past the decimal point? Same thing.

$222 ÷ $367 = .60~~4904632~~ means $222 ÷ $367 = .60 OR 60%

Your imaginary spending on food according to this is 60% of your Flexible Spending. Do this with all three categories to find your personal Flexible Spending scores.

F ÷ tfsbb = percent $ __________ ÷ ___________ = . ___ ___ or ___ ___ %
FOOD / Total Before Budget / Long number – reduced to two digits

C ÷ tfsbb = percent $ __________ ÷ ___________ = . ___ ___ or ___ ___ %
CLOTHING / Total Before Budge / Long number – reduced to two

E ÷ tfsbb = percent $ __________ ÷ ___________ = . ___ ___ or ___ ___ %
ENTERTAINMENT / Total Before Budget Same Number each time / Long number – reduced to two

You CAN keep those percentage numbers for your spending plan. But since you're trying to teach yourself to BUDGET your expenses, look back at the lists on Flexible Spending Pt 1 and see if there are some choices you made that you can change now that you're TRYING to sort it all out in favor of saving more.

Do you think you'll need to allocate your money differently? Is Entertainment more important than Food? Or, is Clothing more important than Entertainment? It's up to you! Remember Kheruef reminded Qishti in the story that he does not have to make himself a slave to the numbers … because he is managing the budget!

Create a Budget - Flexible Spending Pt 3 Name ____________________________

Now you have three percentages. I'm going to use the example, imaginary percentages to show you how this can work.

Moving from "Before Budget" to just the Total Flexible Spending in your Budget
Our imaginary friend on the previous worksheet spent 60% on FOOD, 24% on CLOTHING and 16% on ENTERTAINMENT. He'd really rather be able to go out with his friends more and he wants to increase his ENTERTAINMENT portion. He decided to downshift on his FOOD to 50%, because he *read this book and decided that should, theoretically, be enough*! Hahaha! He now has 10% of his $367 dollar total (tfsbb) to move around – or $36.70. He adds 10% to his ENTERTAINMENT and now he's got:

FOOD 50% CLOTHING 24% ENTERTAINMENT 26%

Your Actual Budget
Look at **your numbers** and decide if you want to keep them the same or adjust some of the percentages.

FOOD _____% CLOTHING ______% ENTERTAINMENT _____%

To figure out his total cash allowance, he'll need to multiply

(50%) $367 x .50; (24%) $367 x.24; (26%) and $367 x.26.

F = $367 x .50 = $183.50	C = $367 x .24 = $88.08	E = $367 x .26 = $95.42
Total % Amount of …	Total % Amount of …	Total % Amount of …

Do the same now with your own numbers.

F = $______ x .______ = $ _______

C = $______ x . _____ = $ ________

E = $______ x .______ = $ ________

You now have the amount of money that you have decided you can spend on FOOD, CLOTHING, and ENTERTAINMENT in your new Budget!

Congratulations!
You're ALMOST done with budgeting!

Create a Budget – The Point of it All Name ______________________________

The WHOLE POINT of creating YOUR OWN PERSONAL BUDGET is that you learn to follow it! So, it's time for some reflection.

Look back at the Worksheet - **Creating a Budget** – The Flexible Spending Pt 1. Some of you already know that you're going to be looking at those lists, AND the CREDIT CARD and BANK STATEMENTS. Those expenditures – that's you … doing what you feel like doing.

And, quite possibly, it's NOT THE BEST THAT YOU CAN DO! You can probably DO BETTER. Which of the things on those lists do you think you COULD have done without? That second cup of coffee at Starbucks on the same day? That round of beer you bought for EVERYONE? That totally cute underwear that you only wear SOMETIMES? That tie that looked like your boss's tie so you could impress him?

And, look again – How many of those purchases are TOTALLY YOU? The tickets you scored to the concert of the year? That mani/pedi date you went on with your best friends? That midnight pizza you ordered when your sister/brother stopped by?

Prepare the following lists based on what you've learned about how you make choices.

Time to Make Some Informed Choices.

Now, it's time to start doing the hard work of fashioning your Financial Self the same way you fashion your Physical Self and your Social Self. And you need to do it with time, love, patience, and care for yourself going in a new direction. Do you absolute best to try NOT TO SPEND every last penny in your budget so that you'll have some rollover money left in your account …. For that emergency. Just sayin'.

Things I can do without MOST of the time:	Things I LOVE TO DO, but shouldn't make a bad habit of doing:

Create a Budget – The Allowance Name ______________________________

Go back to the end of Flexible Spending - Doing the Math.

At the end of that worksheet you discovered your Flexible Spending Amount. And, let's say for argument's sake that the BUDGET and/or SPENDING PLAN just "isn't you."

In the story, Kheruef gives his class the Allowance Plan – simpler times, I guess.

Take the number you got for your Flexible Spending amount and divide it by four for the average four weeks in a month. I'll give an example here.

Let's say our imaginary friend came up with $367.00. He notices that the month has 4 weeks in it this time (sometimes there are 5 weeks) so, he knows to divide $367.00 by 4 weeks to figure out how much he can spend total each week – ON EVERYTHING from FOOD to CLOTHES to ENTERTAINMENT.

$367.00 ÷ 4 (wks) = allowance per week $367.00 ÷ 4 (wks) = $91.75

Do that now with your own amounts in the equations.

$_______ ÷ 4 (wks) = allowance per week $_______ ÷ 4 (wks) = $_________

The trick is staying within your allotted amount.

This means, you STILL need to do the Worksheet **Creating A Budget – The Point of it ALL**. You STILL need to think about what is important to you so you can begin to manage your money instead of letting the desire-of-the-moment overtake you.

How can you do this?

1) Possibly, pull out the money, put it in 4 envelopes and keep that one envelope on you for one whole week. The best part of this is that you can see IMMEDIATELY when you're running low and slow down.

2) Put ALL OF YOUR FLEXIBLE SPENDING money in your SAVINGS ACCOUNT and transfer into your checking account ONLY the amount for the week. The good thing here is that

for a very short period of time, your money in the savings account is earning a wee bit (really wee) of interest. It works if you use your debit card. This is also only a good idea IF you actually check your account in between transfer days (say, Sundays) to see when you're running low. ON TOP OF THAT, it's ONLY GOOD if your bank doesn't have a "low amount in checking account" fee. Better check on that .

3) This is probably best for someone who has simple needs and desires ... like making it through the week without overspending. And that COULD be YOU!!

Good Luck!

Invest in Your Home and Family Pt 1 Name ______________________________

The idea of investing isn't the sole property of money. If you invest energy into a project, the return is a sense of self-worth and a project completed. If you invest emotional energy in a relationship, many times that pays off in more intimacy and trust. If you invest spiritual energy in yourself, there is a sense of completeness and belonging. And sometimes, you invest energy in this or that and it doesn't look as though it pays off until many years later!

Make a list of things you think you can invest **energy** on in relation to your home and family.

________________________________ ________________________________

________________________________ ________________________________

________________________________ ________________________________

You can also invest time in something. Instead of "spending time" – which implies that once you're "spent" you will have no more time – try investing your time in something, someone, or yourself. Investing implies there will be a reward or pay back down the road. If you spend time exercising your back and core muscles, down the road, you are likely to suffer from back problems when you're older.

Make a list of things you can invest **time** on in relation to your home and family. (Make sure to invest time in sleeping ... not kidding!)

________________________________ ________________________________

________________________________ ________________________________

________________________________ ________________________________

Reflect on your choices. Invest in the time it takes to consider who you are and what you really want in life. Make time for yourself every day to think. Go outside and think. Meditate, or at the very least, become mindful of your environments.

Pay attention to the things you pay attention to. What makes you smile? What makes you cry? What makes you genuinely laugh, even guffaw? What makes you turn up the radio/TV? What makes you turn it down or off? (The choice of Radio/TV is intentional here because if you only listen to your own music, there's no real sense of serendipity or something unexpected coming on.)

Things I STOPPED to **pay attention to.**

Pay Attention
To the
THINGS
You Pay
Attention To.

Invest in Your Home and Family Pt 2 Name ______________________________

You put away your coins into a savings account, and when you can, you put away more than just the 10%. That savings account serves as a buffer in times of need – say, new tires for those old bald ones that are just flat out dangerous. It sits and sits and sits and money accrues – at least that's the hope. When comes that day, the money could serve as a down payment on property that you will OWN. Yes, you'll probably have to borrow some of the money, but having money to put down means better financing, lower payments, etc.

You can invest in a home or condo for yourself, OR you can buy rental properties right way. You can purchase land with an idea of selling it later or building on it. You can buy industrial real estate where individuals and companies set up business, or you can buy commercial real estate (motels, strip malls, offices, etc.) in town with an eye toward redeveloping it. Or, you can decide to upgrade and modify your existing home.

Imagine that you've have collected enough "coins" to do some investing, like the examples above. What do you think you'd like to do?

____

____

____

____

Look at the above as your goal. What do you need to learn in order to move smoothly into your plan?

____

____

____

____

____

The more you plan for the eventuality of this happening, the easier the transition will be. So, now, think of where you could go to learn these skills. It could be as simple as YouTube! Or, it could be more complex like taking a class at a night school or trade school.

____

____

____

____

And finally, what can you practice doing now? Feel like learning how to change out a toilet and could do it in your current living circumstance? Want to learn how to grow a porch garden? Then, go for it!

____

____

____

Prepare for the Future Name ______________________________

Investing money in CD's, or the stock market, or bonds is done by opening an investment account. To do that, you can go solo by opening your own brokerage account, or you can do it through some sort of an advisor (robo or human) who guides your purchases.

In either case, you will need to learn the language. There are PLENTY of wonderful and not so wonderful websites out there. Some are free and some you must join and others charge a fee. You decide.
Here are just a few!

https://www.nerdwallet.com

https://www.investopedia.com

https://www.thestreet.com

https://www.forbes.com

https://www.moneyunder30.com

https://www.listenmoneymatters.com

https://smartasset.com

https://www.investor.gov This is the website for the U.S. Securities and Exchange Commission

Don't forget! **Libraries** have books on investing that you can check out - free. And **bookstores** – yes, some still exist – have books and workbooks on investing, so you can WRITE in your own book! You can also go to places like Kindle/Amazon and find eBooks. (or wherever you go for your favorite eBook seller!)

About the Author

Diane Koster has been in education for 37 years in a variety of capacities. She taught in an adult business school, at an outdoor science school, at private and public elementary, middle and high schools. She also served as a reading coach in a special reading lab for adults and children with reading disabilities. Her many hobbies include reading – especially non-fiction, science and new children's books – as well as gardening, hiking and knitting.

Made in the USA
Coppell, TX
04 November 2026

11287994R00063